T0086314

PLAIN JANE

My Wonderfully Ordinary Life

Hannah Jane White/Gregory W. McClinchey

PLAIN JANE
MY WONDERFULLY ORDINARY LIFE

iUniverse books may be ordered through booksellers or by contacting:

iUniverse
1663 Liberty Drive
Bloomington, IN 47403
www.iuniverse.com
844-349-9409

ISBN: 978-1-6632-2929-8 (sc)
ISBN: 978-1-6632-3016-4 (hc)
ISBN: 978-1-6632-2930-4 (e)

Library of Congress Control Number: 2021919917

Print information available on the last page.

iUniverse rev. date: 10/23/2021

WITH LOVE AND THANKS TO MY
CHILDREN AND FAMILY

Contents

PREFACE

In 2021, I celebrated my 89th birthday, and like everyone who manages that lofty feat, I took a moment to take stock of all that I've done and seen throughout my life. I know that I have been lucky and blessed, and as a result, I am truly happy. Perhaps it's because I have always been content, and I have never been alone. I had loving parents, a happy childhood, good friends, and an amazing family, and I was married to a wonderful and caring man for 65 years. Together we travelled, raised seven children, and saw the arrival of 15 grandchildren and 23 great-grandchildren (and counting). We always had laughter in our hearts, food on our table, and fire in our furnace. On the whole, I couldn't have wished for more.

But as I reflected, I couldn't help but hear the words of some of my children and grandchildren who urged me to preserve at least a few of my memories and family stories on paper. While I see my life as having been wonderfully ordinary, they see the value in saving parts of the past so that those who come next can share in the laughter, lessons, and even the tears of those stories ... and I agree. I can only hope they will enjoy reading my recollections as much as I enjoyed living them, and then tell them across a family table in the future.

As I reminisced and retold my stories for placement onto the pages of this book, with the help of my granddaughter's husband, Greg, I again thought of people and happenings long since forgotten. I remembered old tales and events from my youth, and I even discovered some family history that was entirely new to me. Looking back, I guess I put all my energy and time into living my life in the moment, and I didn't spend as much time thinking about parts of that life that might one day be interesting or memorable to others. That is, until now. It may not be much, but if I can leave you with anything, I hope to encourage you to enjoy the present before it fades too far into the past.

These following pages contain my stories, told from my perspective, and in my way (with help from Greg). They are meant to be positive and happy not because that is all there was, but because that's what I remember most. I may not get every detail just right, but the heart of each story remains true (and isn't that what telling a good story is all about?). I hope you enjoy the read. I would like to thank everyone who supported me and had a role in what makes the contents of this book so special to me.

Thanks for the memories,

Jane

Chapter 1

A Place to Call Home

May you always walk in sunshine,
May you never want for more,
May Irish angels rest their wings beside your nursery door.
—An Irish Blessing

It was a cold and snow-swept day in January 1932. The hard part of the Canadian winter had arrived. The river was frozen, the fields were bright and shiny white, and the blue crocuses near the house were covered with a thick layer of clear, rippled ice. The daytime temperature of just 8 degrees Fahrenheit was far colder than anything seen back in the old country, but in Southwestern Ontario, it was just another winter day.

The low howl of the near 20-mile-per-hour wind whistled through the spaces between the house and the barn, making it impossible to discern the nickering of the horses from the lowing of the cattle. A warm fire crackled in the kitchen's cookstove, and the smell of woodsmoke was faint in the air. This was a normal scene on the Ovington Family Farm, on the 5th Line of Morris Township (now Huron County Road 16 or Morris Road), but despite the calm and ordinariness of the landscape and times, January 30 of this year was to be a day unlike most others before.

Above: My cousin Sam Ovington and I stand outside the Ovington Family Farm. This simple structure— my first home on the 5th Line of Morris Township— still stands today.

The sun was just starting to rise above the crest of the hill on Art Hull's farm (one of the highest points in Morris Township) when, for the second time in the four years since 1928, Mary Ovington (born Mary Elizabeth Alcock) started to prepare herself for another special arrival. The coming of a new baby was always an important part of life in any homestead and rural community, but the event was not an excuse for the demands and hustle of daily chores to slow for any member of the household. There were meals to be prepared, bedding to be changed, stove-wood to be fetched, and countless other routine household tasks to be planned and finished before more pressing concerns were tackled.

In the meantime, it was a time for daughters to call upon mothers and sisters to lend a hand with both the immediate running of the home and the actual delivery of the new family member. As was the typical practice in rural Ontario at the time, a lengthy trip by horse-drawn cutter to the closest hospital was out of the question. These were the days before standardized and publicly funded health care had arrived in the province, so the added cost of a hospital visit meant that a home birth would be the order of the day.

2

Home births may have been the norm, but they were not without some level of anxious anticipation and even risk for all involved. Birth and infant mortality rates in rural Ontario at the time were high, hovering on the dark side of 12 per cent, so careful planning, and as much luck as this simple Irish home could muster, would be key.

Word was sent to Dr. Jameson (no known connection to Dublin's own Jameson Irish Whiskey), who attended the house but reportedly dashed up and down the concession road to attend to multiple home births over the course of the day. To augment the doctor's somewhat fragmented focus, Mary Ovington's mother, Mary Jane Alcock, and sister, Annie Bernard, served as doulas and ensured that appropriate hot water, clean towels, fresh bedding, and other essentials were available when and if the doctor called for them.

But first, Mary, her mother, and her sister began fixing hearty meals for the day, gathering supplies, and preparing for the labours ahead. If all went well, by the time evening chores were done, Samuel Jacob Ovington would, as a father for the second time, have cause to raise a glass of sharp Irish whiskey in celebration.

In my first act of rebelliousness, adhering strictly to my own timetable, my arrival happened much later in the day than my mother had anticipated. It was well into the evening when I made my debut into what was to be my first home. By all accounts, I was loud, energetic, healthy, and above all, content. These traits were already present on Day One and, as it turned out, they would continue and serve me well throughout both the hardest and the happiest times of my life to come.

Above: Me, Baby Hannah Jane Ovington, on one of my earliest days

On this particular Saturday evening, with all the luck of the Irish, I found my way into my mother's arms in a modest home that, despite the normal imperfections and financial limitations of the day, was filled with love and all the necessities I would need to grow and prosper. While present-day judgments might say that we were poor, as I remember it, we always had just enough.

Above: My brother, Tony Ovington, circa 1932

My brother, Tony—just 4 years old at the time and named after our uncle Tony Ovington, who died in France at the Battle of the Somme in WWI on November 13, 1916—was immediately smitten with his tiny new baby sister, and that special sibling bond would hold for the remainder of his days. But Tony wasn't the only one who was excited. I was later told that my mother openly imagined the days ahead with a little helper tugging at her apron strings. She finally had the wee girl she had always wanted—but I have often wondered if she had any inkling that the delicate flower she envisioned was to be a somewhat rugged tomboy who enjoyed the outdoors and other activities most often attributed to boys in those days. Years later, she would have to admit that I was as rough-and-tumble as the Wicklow hills.

Then there was Daddy. On a normal Saturday night at this time, he would have been well along, sitting in the pub down the road in Brussels. But that night, he stuck close to home. I would later come to hear that Daddy beamed in that way that fathers do when presented with their darling little girl for the very first time. Neither of us knew it at that moment, but regardless of what the future would hold, I had already cooed and wiggled into the vein of his rough Irish heart.

Looking back, I like to imagine Daddy sitting quietly beside the fire that winter evening, relaxed in his chair, pipe clenched in his teeth, with the newest Ovington swaddled in his arms. Perhaps he quietly smiled as he dozed and looked away into the distance, thinking of all that had passed, as the pipe smoke wafted around his relatively young but work-worn face. We were a world away from the violence, hardships, and instability of the Ireland of his youth, but things were already quite different. Daddy must have known that the years ahead would be filled with challenges, hardship, loss, success, happiness, and triumph.

On that day, though, his sacrifices and long journey from County Wicklow to Huron County must have seemed somehow worthwhile. He had left his home, friends, neighbours, siblings, and parents behind. He had plunged into the unknown. But because of his stubborn determination and adventurous nature, his young family was now settled, content, and complete, and my adventure was set to begin.

CHAPTER 2

A FAMILY FOUNDATION

*A family of Irish birth will argue and fight, but let a shout
come from without and see them unite.—An Irish Proverb*

For hundreds of years, Ireland has been known as the Emerald Isle
because of its lush green landscapes. Most know this from books and
movies, but the reality of the label struck me especially when I first
visited Ireland with my husband, Clarence (and our daughter Judy;
her husband, Ross; and their children), in 1990. Even during that
brief visit, it was easy to see why Ireland is said to be green. In fact, as
has been pointed out to me since, this greenery helped to shape Irish
culture, folklore, and farming traditions that date back to well beyond
living memory.

As it had been for generations before, in the early 1900s, my father,
grandfather, and most of their friends and neighbours were entirely
dependent on farming for their survival and for any hope of future
prosperity. Daily life in those days would have been back-breaking
already, but the beginning of the 1900s would have been especially
hard for any working-class Irish family. It was into this time and place
that my daddy, Samuel Jacob Ovington, started his journey—and, by
extension, it is where my own life first started to put down roots.

Daddy was born on a warm spring day, April 28, 1898, on the
family farm at Woodfield, near Baltinglass, nestled in the Wicklow
hills just 60 kilometres south of Dublin. His childhood was short

and simple compared to what we expect and hope for our children today. In those days, there was little time, and even less money, for the kinds of extracurricular activities enjoyed by my own grandchildren and, to a lesser extent, my children. Organized sports and extravagant holidays were unheard of in those days. Young children would have been expected to start contributing labour to the family farm and household as soon as they were physically able—for many, even before their teen years had started. While the theory of this approach is that many hands make lighter work, in those days, there really was no such thing as light work.

Above: Daddy was always a dapper and handsome fellow.

Daddy, his parents (Anthony Ovington and Eleanor Glynn), and his eight siblings—Elizabeth, Richard, Mary Ann (Minnie), Joseph, Anthony, Robert, Ellen, and Jacob (who died in infancy)—were born and existed in a world shaped by turmoil, unrest, and general scarcity. Things were scant when I was a little girl, but in the days of Daddy's youth, things were even tighter. Put plainly, poverty and hardship were the norm for many in those days, and constant hard work was the only hope one could have of staving off hunger, sickness, and general disaster.

Even though the Ovington family lived what must have seemed like a world away from the strife of the crowded streets of large cities like Dublin, it would have been impossible for them to entirely escape the serious financial, social, and political problems of Irish life during in the early 1900s. This is because Ireland at the turn of the twentieth century was a place with lots of good people facing lots of terrible struggles. Despite the hard times, I am sure that no one could have imagined the island was perched on the edge of change that would shake nearly ever bit of their daily life. The winds of change blew lightly at first but gathered steam as the months and years rolled on. The troubles started in Dublin, but soon enough, they spilled out of the city, past the suburbs, and squarely onto the backs of Irish farmers in places like Baltinglass.

It all started with one of the most serious labour disruptions in Irish history. Daddy was just a teenager when, in August of 1913, the Dublin Lockout exploded into a mess that saw months of street violence, thousands of workers fired, hundreds of businesses shuttered, and eventually, a crash in the already shaky farming economy. This was all happening at a time when thousands of young men and women were being struck down each year with diseases like tuberculosis and pneumonia, largely because of the tough working and living conditions.

As if that wasn't bad enough, the Dublin Lockout was followed by the Easter Rising in 1916, the Conscription Crisis of 1918, and the onset of the 1919 War of Independence. As a result of the seemingly endless violence and unrest, even those with regular work found life to be precarious. An entire generation of Irish youth, including Samuel Ovington, would have faced a dismal future with only faint hopes of making their own way unless they were prepared to take drastic action.

If I try to put myself into Daddy's shoes, it must have been dreadful. Just as Daddy would have been thinking about his own working future and starting a family, these developments would have upended everything he knew and counted on. Although there is no way to know for sure, it is almost certain that the poverty and want of those lean times shaped Daddy, from his earliest days, into a young man who would imagine, and eventually seek, a better life across the Atlantic in Canada. After all, for the entire span of his young life—from his birth until at least his twenties—Ireland faced wave after wave of violence, unrest, and change that would have hindered his ability to find stability and prosperity. It is impossible to think this would not have had an impact on him and those around him.

It was against this backdrop that, on June 6, 1924, at just 25 years of age, Samuel Jacob Ovington and his older brother Joseph (Joe) decided to take hold of their own futures and set sail for North America. The brothers purchased third-class fare aboard the Canadian Pacific steamship *Montclare* and embarked from the English port of Liverpool with the hope of finding greener pastures when they landed in the Canadian province of Quebec. Presumably, Joe had arrived at the same conclusion regarding his future job prospects in Ireland, opting to say goodbye to his childhood home, friends, and neighbours. He eventually established his family in the American city of Kalamazoo, Michigan.

The Ovington Family diaspora would grow yet again some years later, on February 2, 1928, when Daddy's younger brother Robert (Bob) Ovington boarded the Canadian Pacific steamship *Melita* and joined his brothers in the Americas. Daddy and his brothers had each in turn come to understand that money and jobs were in short supply in Ireland and the prospect of things getting better in the short-term was unlikely at best. It was also probable, given that they were children no longer, that my grandfather would have felt it was time for them to start making plans for families and lives of their own. In essence, the Ovington brothers had come to the point in their lives when they needed to put their boots under their own tables, so to speak.

In his youth, Daddy had a somewhat wild temperament and spent his fair share of time in the pub with his pals. As one might expect, drink occasionally collided with his fiery Irish temper and boiled over, as was more the norm than the exception for rough-and-tumble young men in those days. This and some other normal sibling rivalries meant that Daddy and his older brother Anthony (Tony) didn't always get on. This is not to suggest that they disliked each other, but as brothers can be, they were each other's best of friends and sparring partners rolled into one. Because of this rivalry, and because extended families needed to take care of each other in those days, my grandfather sent Daddy to live with his mother's spinster sister Hannah. By the social standards of the early 1900s, Daddy was more than old enough to work hard and to help look after both Aunt Hannah and her small farm.

As I understand it, Daddy's time with Aunt Hannah was not at all unpleasant. While he was certainly expected to earn his keep at the point of a plough, this was also the time when he left behind his life as a child. As a young man with his own mind and a strong will, he started to make future plans and to develop into the man he was to become. For example, it was at this point that Daddy joined the Church via his Confirmation of Faith on May 18, 1913. Faith was certainly a big part of Irish life in those days.

Above: Daddy's Confirmation of Faith card, signed by Stuart Long, rector of the church (part of the United Dioceses of Dublin) in 1913. Daddy was a good Christian man who always made sure we attended church on Sunday mornings.

Daddy and Aunt Hannah's relationship was generally a good one, as at least in part evidenced by him eventually deciding to name me after her (and also my maternal grandmother Mary Jane). Notwithstanding the positives of living with Aunt Hannah, there still comes a time when any Irish lad needs to transform the sweat of his own brow into adventure, and eventually into prosperity. By mid-1924, that call must have been impossible for Daddy to ignore.

As the summer heat of 1924 arrived, Daddy and Uncle Joe decided to leave their small Wicklow home in the Emerald Isle behind. Daddy had managed to somehow gather up an impressive amount of money by that time. The official landing documents that he filled out when he arrived in Canada confirmed that he had fifty pounds in his pocket at the time of his arrival. This impressive amount of money would have been his entire life savings to that point and probably all that his parents could lend him. That seed money would have been his only insurance policy as he set out to start his new life alone in Canada.

As I understand it, Daddy's father and mother were less than fully enthusiastic to say goodbye, especially as it meant their boys would probably be forever leaving their home and country behind. The family had already lost children—Jacob in infancy and Anthony during the 1916 Battle of the Somme—so I suspect they were not keen to lose any more family members. Irish families moving to North America for work was normal in those days, but it must still have been a tough pill to swallow for any parent.

I look at my own family, and I can't imagine saying goodbye to any of them. In my mind, Daddy's parents would have resisted and tried everything they could to dissuade the move, but truthfully, it was probably for the best given the job prospects at home. At any rate, necessity's pull proved stronger than parental resistance. Daddy and Joe packed their modest belongings—just what they could carry—and set out from Liverpool toward North America, and onward to the future.

The duo landed at the Port of Quebec and eventually worked their way westward into central Canada. The available records indicate that Joe probably went to the United States straight away, while Daddy headed like a bolt for Ontario. Daddy visited Joe in March of 1925, but it is clear that, while Joe set up shop in Kalamazoo, Daddy arrived in Canada with a plan to make his way toward the fertile fields of Southwestern Ontario. Presumably, this plan was driven by the promise of stable work.

Daddy's official "Declaration of Passenger to Canada" document makes his plans clear. In his own hand (Daddy could both read and write), he wrote that he intended to stay in Canada "To Settele" (sic), and the document confirmed that he was destined for the Alcock farm in Brussels, Ontario. As the story was told to me, Daddy knew of this

Irish family who had moved to Ontario and now farmed. As a self-identified farm labourer, Daddy must have seen real opportunity in the vast openness of the territory, especially with a live-in job promised by the wife of RB Alcock as a real income while he worked to establish himself in his new country and community.

❦

Richard Beacham (RB) Alcock, who was probably not directly known to Daddy or to the Ovington family before Daddy moved to Canada, was born on August 2, 1863, in Grey Township, Ontario, but his family originally hailed from Antrim. Located in County Antrim, Antrim is a civil parish in Northern Ireland about 60 kilometres from Baltinglass. The distance from Antrim to Baltinglass would suggest that the two families probably did not know each other, but as Antrim was serviced by rail as early as 1848, it is possible that RB Alcock or his family could have traversed the distance and somehow met the Ovingtons while still in Ireland.

Although there is no indication or documented record of such an encounter, it is also worth noting that RB's maternal family had roots in Carlow, a community located just 25 kilometres west of Baltinglass and less than 10 kilometres from Aunt Hannah's farm. This closer geography means it is at least possible that the Alcock family and the Ovington family had encountered each other prior to RB and his family making their transatlantic move.

What is known is that at some point after the Alcock family left Ireland, and after RB's birth in Grey Township, Ontario, Canada, the family moved to a small rural municipality in southwestern Ontario then known as Morris Township. That municipality was situated in the northern portion of Huron County, near to the Bruce County border, southeast of the town of Wingham. It is today known as Morris-Turnberry and even now has a population of fewer than four thousand people. In the early 1900s, the entire population of the township was only a few hundred people, and there were no cities, large towns, or government services of note.

In every sense of it, the area was part of a central Canadian frontier that promised opportunity for those who were ready to roll up their sleeves. I expect that a young man with little to lose would have seen this journey as exciting, but life would have been hard without friends or close family supports to speak of. I guess this is probably why the Alcock connection was so important in those early days and ended up being a permanent element of Daddy's life.

On the other side of the family tree, Mary Jane Alcock (same last name but no relationship to RB's paternal line) was born on August 17, 1861, to George Alcock and Jane Glynn in Kiltegan, a small farming community just 8 kilometres south-east of Baltinglass. I suspect, given the closer proximity of the Ovington and Alcock family homes, that Mary Jane or her family may have been known to the Ovington family in Ireland. This notion would seem to be verified by the fact that Daddy's original 1924 "Declaration of Passenger to Canada" specifically identified "Mrs. Alcock" (RB's wife) as his contact in Canada. If this is the case, this association would be the connection that eventually led Daddy to seek out work in Ontario.

As an aside, Mary Jane Alcock's family home was a modest but solidly built two-storey cement house. So solid was the construction of the home that, even though it has been empty for decades, the tough wee structure still stands in the Mungoduff (locally pronounced "Mugduff"), Kiltegan, County Wicklow. I had the chance to visit the old Alcock family home in 1990, and both Clarence and I were amazed to see just how well it had weathered all those years.

Above: My husband, Clarence, and my aunt Mary Anne Ovington (Uncle Bob's wife) stand near Grandma Alcock's family home, as it looks today, in Mungoduff.

As a young maid, Mary Jane Alcock moved to southern Ontario and eventually married RB Alcock on September 9, 1892. The couple made their home on various farms in Grey and Morris townships, where they had seven children, including a daughter in January of 1905 who would eventually become my mother, Mary Elizabeth Alcock. Their final family home was to be on the 5th Line of Morris Township (now know as Huron County Road 16).

❦

The Ovington brothers seemingly enjoyed their new home and stuck it out for several years until, in December of 1927, Daddy decided to pay his parents and Irish family a visit. While no one knows for sure why he decided to make the trip, Daddy's older sister Ellen had died of tuberculosis a few months earlier, and it had recently been the anniversary of Uncle Anthony's death in World War I, so the timing would have been appropriate for a family reconnect and a shared commiseration. It was also Christmas, so the homecoming may just have been as simple as a yuletide visit. But I suspect there may have been a more pressing matter of family business to share. After all, my brother, Tony, was born in May of 1928, and Daddy would have been excited to share news of the pending birth with his parents and extended family.

Regardless of the reason, a transatlantic crossing was still complicated and even a little risky in those days. Making the trip from Canada to Ireland in the 1920s was expensive and could take as long as two weeks each way depending on the time of year and the weather. Added to the actual crossing time was the journey from Huron County to the departure port, which was no small feat in and of itself, even to one as close as Sarnia, Ontario. There was also the lost time from work and the corresponding wage losses to be considered as part of the trip cost during a period when money was already tight. With all of this in mind, the trip to Ireland was not a journey that one made often or without good reason and careful consideration. Given all of this, it seems that the pull of family must have been especially strong for Daddy.

With that trip, fate made yet another move, and the unity of the family was temporarily changed again. Daddy stayed in Ireland for a couple of months before returning to Canada, but this time he brought his brother Robert (Bob) as a travelling companion. While eventually Uncle Bob was enticed to return to Ireland by his father's gift of a threshing machine and the promise it provided as a source of a real income and opportunity, on February 13, 1928, after an 11-day voyage across the Atlantic, Daddy and Bob arrived in St. John, New Brunswick, together. There was now an extra Ovington on Canadian soil.

While Uncle Bob eventually returned to Ireland to raise his own family, Joe continued with his life in the United States, and Daddy held fast with his plans of settling permanently in Canada. You see, Daddy was a determined man who did not change his mind easily. I suppose that is a nice way of saying he was stubborn, a personality trait that would both define him and serve him as he worked to carve out his new life in Canada. By 1928, his mind was made up and his path was clear. Notwithstanding the fact that he had married my mother in 1926, little had changed in Ireland to keep him there, and his gaze was fixed upon Canada and his Canadian family. Certain off-handed family stories from way back suggest that Daddy had commenced his courtship with my mother well before it was official, but by the late 1920s, those stories had long-since been put to rest.

Daddy's gainful work digging ditches with RB Alcock's sons and their team of Clydesdales was a strong anchor for a dream that had been several years in the making. While I may never know for sure if it was a quest for adventure, romance, an economic necessity, or even some of each, his decision to remain in Canada stood. All of this had set into motion a chain of events that would cause him to move in with RB and Mary Jane Alcock, to meet their young daughter and his future wife, to acquire ownership of the Alcock homestead on the 5th of Morris, and to become a father of his own son, Anthony (fondly named after the older brother killed in WWI), in 1928, and of me (named after the aunt he lived with as a teen and for the mother-in-law who helped welcome him to Canada) in 1932.

Daddy was finally able to put down more permanent roots and to build a life and family of his own. It could be said that this phase of his life officially started in 1926, when Daddy and my mother were married in a simple ceremony in the Brussels Anglican Church, but I think the story starts much earlier. Looking back, Daddy's sacrifices and hard work certainly paved my way and the way for my children, grandchildren, and great-grandchildren. Daddy would later quip that, although his long road from Wicklow had been winding and bumpy, the view at the end made it all more than worth the trip.

❦

It is important to know that, although troubled times and circumstances would separate the Ovington brothers, and even the extended Ovington family, for decades, that last visit home was not to be the final chapter in the relationship between Daddy, Joseph, and Robert Ovington or their descendants. While that familial relationship would be paused (aside from letters and occasional face-to-face visits) for many years, the brothers stayed connected as much as they could in a world before e-mail and long-distance calling.

On one such occasion in 1956, Joseph and his wife, Gladys, made the trip from Kalamazoo to visit with Daddy and our family in Ontario. While the timing of the visit coincided with a two-year bout of ill health for Daddy, and it occurred in Beck Memorial Hospital in Byron, the brotherly connection was intact and easy to see. That face-to-face meeting is something that I remember still. Uncle Joe was like a long-lost friend—a missing piece to our family puzzle. He brought gifts for my three oldest children (Sid, Judy, and Rick) and regaled us with the other half of Daddy's stories from times long passed.

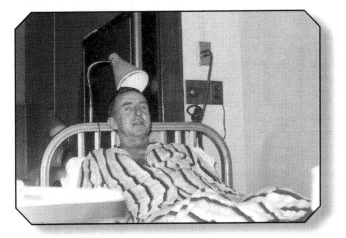

Above: Daddy during his lengthy stay at Beck Memorial Hospital in Byron.

Years later, in 1990, my husband, Clarence, and I took a trip to Ireland with our oldest daughter, Judy; her husband, Ross Somers; and their two children, Scott and Heather. We had an interesting and memorable stay at Germaine's in Baltinglass and enjoyed visiting the pubs and walking the paths Daddy would have trod as a youngster. As an aside, Germaine's came to be a special place for us, and we went back often—so often, in fact, that Clarence even had his own designated stool at the bar.

During that first adventure, we started to rekindle our long-lost family relationships, including those with Uncle Bob's line across the generations. That first trip turned into more and, over time, our family ties strengthened. Meeting Aunt Mary Anne Ovington (Uncle Bob's wife), Anthony, Nelly, Daphne, Noel, Sam, Richard, and their family members helped to close the family gap my grandparents must have feared all those years earlier.

Above: Clarence and I welcome Noel and Helen Ovington to our home in Wingham, Ontario. Noel is Uncle Bob's son.

Our later trips to Ireland in 1997, 2000, and 2005 were reciprocated by many visits to Canada by extended Irish family members. Later still, my children, grandchildren, and even my great-grandchildren visited Ireland and established and maintained family connections of their own across the Atlantic. All of this has allowed us to pick up where Daddy and his brothers left off in the 1920s and to again unite as a family.

Above: Uncle Bob's wife, Aunt Mary Anne; Mary Anne's second husband, Tom Moorehouse; and Uncle Bob's four sons and two daughters gather together in Ireland in 1999.

As I sit here today, looking at old pictures and thinking about how much has changed for our family since Daddy's journey began back in 1924, I can't help but be happy that the Ovingtons have reconnected and gotten to know each other again. Getting to know my own cousins and their extended families, and having their families get to know my children, grandchildren, and great-grandchildren, is a wonderful thing for all of us. It seems that there is indeed truth to the saying that, even when separated by years, time spent with family is worth every second.

Chapter 3

The Apple Tree

*One of the luckiest things that can happen to you in life is,
I think, to have a happy childhood.—Agatha Christie*

As a young and spirited child, I spent loads of time on a rickety homemade swing that hung from an old rope looped over the branches of an apple tree in our yard at home. That farm, on the 5th Line of Morris Township, is often what I see when I close my eyes and let my mind wander. It's where I was born, and it was the only home I would know until I moved to the Blyth Hotel to work as a housekeeper for a couple of months in 1948, at the tender age of 16.

The farm was home to three generations of my family and had previously been owned by my maternal grandfather, Richard Beacham (RB) Alcock, a man I heard a lot about but never actually met. After Daddy and my mother were married in 1926, Daddy took on the farm, and it was home for all of us until my parents eventually sold it in 1949 and moved first to another farm near Listowel, in Alma Township, and eventually 15 kilometres north to a little house in Wroxeter where they lived for many years.

Above: Daddy (pipe clenched in his teeth) and my mother on our home farm on the 5th Line of Morris Township, standing in the yard with Daddy's friend Jack. There always seemed to be extra hands around our farm.

At that point, my brother, Tony, and I had moved on to our own lives, in other homes, and my mother's parents were gone, so there was no reason (other than nostalgia) to stay on the farm any longer. Despite all of the changes in my life since then, that old apple-tree swing in the yard has always been memorable for me. In part, it may have been important because, even as a toddler, I relished the feeling of freedom that came from cutting through the air, wind at my face, laughing all the way up from my toes.

When I was planted on the seat of that swing, I had it all. That swing allowed me to have the excitement and independence I wanted while remaining tethered and close to what was important, under the watchful eye of my mother and her mother, Mary Jane Alcock.

Above: My mother, standing outside of Beck Memorial Hospital in Byron, Ontario, in 1956. Mother needed to find work when Daddy was sick, so she used her cooking skills in the hospital kitchen. She did what she loved and was able to be with Daddy when he needed her most.

My mother was a genuine and giving woman who was always kind to family, neighbours, and strangers alike. As a mother, wife, and member of the community, her generosity was as endless as her energy. When I think back on her ways, I can say that no matter how little we had, she seemed perfectly content and even happy with nothing other than her family and friends around her. She and Daddy had that in common.

My mother shared when she had so little—even when the act of giving put her in a perilous spot. She cared for us and for her own parent's right to the end of their time, and throughout all of it, I am not sure I even remember so much as a frown or discouraging word from her regarding our circumstances. Her father RB died in May of 1929, at 66 years of age, but her mother lived until 1942 and age 81. Even when her parents' health faltered and eventually failed, my mother kept them and happily tended to their every need and want.

Grandma was very hands-on when I was growing up, but later, she developed serious dementia, perhaps Alzheimer's disease (we didn't know about Alzheimer's in those days), that robbed her of her mind and precious memories. As her faculties faded, the task of caring for her became increasingly demanding for my mother, and in many ways, for our entire community.

I say this about the community because, on more than one occasion, Grandma wandered off alone, traversing several miles before being found by a friend or neighbour. Fortunately, we lived in a place where most neighbours knew most everything about all the other neighbours, for better and for worse. This familiarity—which was partly because of the close nature of the community and partly because all the houses on the concession were served by the same party-line telephone system—cut both ways depending on the day. But when it came to Grandma wandering off alone, having a close network was a very good thing.

Everyone on the concessions knew to be on the lookout and to let Daddy or my mother know if they saw Grandma Alcock out for a walk by herself. It was not especially uncommon to find Grandma deep in conversation, teacup and saucer in hand, at the home of a friendly neighbour and in need of a ride home to a house she now only vaguely recalled during these hazy spells. Daddy would always go pick her up with the team, or in later years with the car, and my mother would welcome her home with a distant yet familiar smile.

This went on for many years until, on a cloudy and grey day in August of 1942, Grandma Alcock slipped peacefully away. When she passed, we were all hit hard by the loss—especially her ever-faithful companion, a black and white dog named Lassie. The mutt seemed to instinctively know she was gone forever when it curled up near her chair and peacefully followed her. I was just 10 years old at the time, and this coincidental occurrence of loyalty struck me as an amazing connection and a fitting tribute to how important Grandma was to us all.

Above: Daddy's team (Pete and Fred) were tireless and endlessly useful on the farm. They were known to find their own way home on occasions when Daddy had been out socializing and, as a result, was less sure of the route back to the farm.

With Grandma gone, my mother's burden was reduced on the one hand, but she now took on even more of the daily chores around the farm. As recognized by everyone who knew her, Mom faced every situation with a smile and a laugh, and this was no exception. She was always ready to put in the work needed to get any job done, but she staunchly refused to let the busyness of her days take away from her quality time with Tony and me. Her children were clearly important to her. Since Daddy was away often, especially in the evenings, when he could be found at the local pub, my mother stepped up. I see a lot of her in me, and that makes me happy.

My mother milked cows, morning and night; cared for her amazing and well-kept garden; and then transformed all of her products and produce into hearty meals and snacks that were second to none. In hindsight, I came to see that food was just her way of demonstrating love, hospitality, and appreciation. I suppose that is something I inherited from her.

Some days, I can still smell the fresh bread she made from scratch in our old kitchen. When it was warm, Tony and I saw it as a real treat, particularly when we arrived home from school with growling wee bellies. The crust end was always a favourite for both Tony and I, so I guess it was lucky there are two on every loaf.

Mom would cut the fresh bread into thick slices, carefully pack it, and then fill a large basket with vegetables from the garden. She would trail Tony and I down to the river near the laneway, under a tree, for a picnic lunch. Alternatively, when the season was right, we would take our picnic to a small clearing in the bush behind the house. With our honey pails clutched in our tiny hands, we would spend hours filling both our bellies and our buckets with fresh, sweet raspberries from our very own raspberry patch. The berries were better than candy. Our berries were so renowned that sometimes we would catch neighbours sneaking in to help themselves to the juicy red fruit, but most often it was just my mother, Tony, and me.

We would laugh and toddle about, and Mother would even read to us sometimes. I wasn't a big reader at the time, but I sure enjoyed her stories. My mother's voice was easy to listen to, and she told stories like no one else could. Thinking about it now, maybe that is where I got my own storytelling abilities?

These outings were always a favourite for my mother, and we liked them too. Not only was the food fresh, delicious, and hearty, but we got to eat outside, which was where I most wanted to be. In fact, those carefree picnic lunches were some of the happiest times I had with my mother. It was certainly a time when my love of the outdoors fit well with her love of cooking and spending time with her family.

Just as my mother and grandmother were always close at hand in those days, so too was my much quieter older brother, Tony. Looking back, it seems like Tony, ever the good brother, pulled me for miles and miles in our little wagon. He didn't complain about having a little sister trailing along behind him—at least not that I heard or remember. In fact, he didn't say much one way or the other, which was okay with me, because I have never been at a loss for words, nor do I have trouble keeping the conversation going (people tell me this even today). We were best friends and constant playmates in those days. He was always so good to me, even as we got older and left that little wagon behind for other things.

When we were children, Tony would follow me and our dogs Collie and Ginger (and then later our little dog Bruno) across the ploughed fields, or even splash with me in and around the brown mud of the Maitland River that cut through the property between the house and the road near our laneway. We cast our lines off with an old bamboo pole, and Tony would even make rafts with the long grass and debris that washed up each spring. We were wee adventurers, and there was never a shortage of new and interesting things for us to create and explore.

Above: Ginger, Collie, and I take a summer stroll in the river near our laneway (a river that doubled as our bathtub in the summer). The bridge that my grandfather built, and the Ovington Family Farm, can be seen in the background.

In the winter, we would strap on a clunky pair of wooden skis that Daddy had cobbled together for us, and then we would race down the hill on Art Hull's farm (one of the highest points in Morris Township) across the dirt road. It is a wonder that we survived the entire experience without breaking our arms and necks.

We were always looking for the next big thing to try. I remember one cold winter day in particular when Tony and I had the great idea to make a full-size ice rink on the river near the bridge, using our rubber boots for goal markers. Like little muskrats, we burrowed a small hole in the ice and flooded a large patch of our rink-to-be with river water spread about by pail. Our thinking was that the water would freeze hard and fast in the blustery sub-zero temperatures of an Ontario winter night, giving us a perfectly smooth and shiny white surface for our games the next day. It sounded like a grand plan to us, but it didn't completely pan out like we had pictured.

The next morning, after we raced through breakfast and chores, we bundled up and shot off like an arrow to the river as fast as our wee legs could carry us. It wasn't long before our smiles of anticipation turned to frowns as we discovered that our plan had flopped. Instead of a smooth top, an overnight windstorm and a flash freeze in the night had rippled our rink's top. We were disappointed but not defeated, as we managed to find a small patch of rough and uneven ice that we deemed usable enough. It was not the smooth and glassy surface that you find in arenas today, but we didn't care.

We played our own version of Hockey Night in Canada (long before Don Cherry was famous—or infamous) on the ice until the daylight was long gone and our cheeks were deep red. Then, once inside for the night, Tony and I occupied our time with card games and crokinole, a board game invented a few years earlier in neighbouring Perth County (I still enjoy playing crokinole with my neighbours today). Board games were always a mainstay for us because we didn't have a television in those days.

To be honest, we didn't even know what television was; we had never even heard of it. If we were lucky, we might get to hear the crackle of an old battery-powered radio some nights after supper, but usually that was only the news programs Daddy enjoyed. As the radio's battery power was limited, conservation was always important. In other words, Tony and I were not allowed to waste the battery on our shows for fear that Daddy would not be able to hear the all-important nightly newscast. Despite this, and even though I knew better, every now and again after school I would quietly tiptoe into the parlour and listen to *The Adventures of Wild Bill Hickok*. I just loved Wild Bill Hickok. This was a fast-paced half-hour radio western geared to children that I really enjoyed. Daddy never caught me, but only because my mother was willing to keep my secret.

I suppose this was another example of how good I really had it. Looking back, I can see that Daddy and my mother were quite good to us, and I had a streak of mischief that was known to appear on occasion.

Above: My mother and Daddy at home on the farm in Morris Township. My childhood was a happy time.

I always enjoyed music, and music was a big part of life at home. There was an old organ in the house, but no one ever seemed to play it. Instead, from time to time, perhaps on a quiet Saturday evening, the entire family would gather and listen to wrestling, or to the *CKNX Barn Dance* on the radio. Billed as "Canada's Largest Travelling Barn Dance," this musical variety show featured the likes of Serenade Ranch,

Western Roundup, and Circle 8 Ranch. It was always interesting, and I enjoyed the programming, but I also enjoyed the fact that we were all together when it was on.

They may not happen as much today as they once did, but these kinds of together activities were always a hit when I was a little girl. In addition to the regular games that Tony and I played, Daddy and my mother would often join in with us, or even let us go back and forth with friends when time and chore schedules allowed. My mother and Daddy worked hard, but they also liked to kick up their heels, and as a result our house was filled with family, friends, and neighbours every Sunday after lunch. A raucous card game with the neighbours was an entertainment mainstay for Daddy and my mother, and it allowed for the sharing of time, food, and even a nip or two of the good stuff on occasion.

But when we weren't playing board games or listening to our radio programs, Tony and I also spent our fair share of time playing in and around the barn. I liked to spend time in the barn with Daddy because the barn and the barnyard were an endless source of interest and fun. Perhaps our affinity for the place explains why my mother insisted that we keep our cats there—or perhaps she just disliked cats and wanted to keep them at a distance.

I always liked cats, even barn cats. They were great for catching mice and even just as something to watch as they bounced and played about on the thinnest edge of the highest barn beams, but my mother insisted that they were never allowed in the house. I am not exactly sure why. This was unlike her rules for the many white mice, ferrets, and other small critters we smuggled into the house as pets from time to time.

Tony and I were great ones for befriending nearly anything on four legs, whether greyhounds, barn cats, or mice as they skittered around at our feet. I even had a pet pig Mickey for a time, until he suddenly disappeared one day (I suspect that Daddy had a hand in Mickey's disappearance). However, I was then, and I remain, deathly afraid of snakes, so four legs were and are essential for any of my pets.

Above: Tony and I getting into some mischief on the family farm in the late 1930s. The bandage on my foot and the smile on my face would seem to illustrate the rough-and-tumble ways of my youth.

As the years passed, Tony took up hunting and trapping, and I really liked it when he let me come along. After all, what's not to like? Trudging through the muddy fields and bush, checking muskrat traps in the stream, laying belly-down in the wet leaves or brush, and then lugging home a heavy quarry of rabbit for my mother to transform into a delicious stew or freshly made pie. In those days, nothing was wasted, and finding ways to mix work and fun gave us the best of both worlds. You don't see people doing this kind of thing as much today as you did in my youth, although several of my own children and grandchildren are big hunters.

Tony and I were inseparable as children, and we remained close right up to July 18, 2000, when he passed away in the hospital in Listowel. As is normal with siblings, our paths had diverged as we grew older, and as a consequence, we lived very different lives. Despite all that, I have always believed that you should never lose sight of the goodness in people, no matter what. Tony and I became very different people as we grew, but I always loved my big brother dearly and enjoyed each opportunity to visit as it came.

Like me, Tony didn't venture too far from our younger days. Right up to the end, he lived in Brussels, just a short distance from where we played as children. Time was not always kind to Tony, and like Daddy, he struggled with the demons of temper and alcohol, but we were inseparable pals in our early days at home on the farm. Tony was a kind soul and a good brother, and he taught me a lot. He was quiet, but he was always up for an escapade when the mood struck me. I miss him, and sometimes when I am sitting in my big armchair remembering what was, I still think of him and the adventures we would have, and I smile.

◦◦◦

While Tony was my first true friend, he wasn't my only childhood chum. I also had a faithful companion who dutifully followed me without question or complaint everywhere I went. He didn't care that I was sassy or high-spirited, and he certainly didn't shy away from whatever adventure I had dreamed up. His name was Bradley, he was about my age, he had dark and curly hair, and he was probably the most agreeable friend I could have imagined.

In fact, he was actually my imaginary brother, and we had some amazing conversations and adventures together. I suppose I was just a little girl with lots of imagination and, given that I was a bit of a loner and prone to wandering off when Tony wasn't around, I found an ever-ready friend and confidant in Bradley. While eventually I saw less and less of Bradley, I can still vividly picture the face I conjured up for this wonderful little pal. I guess you could say I had a virtual friend before Facebook made it the in thing to do.

I was also lucky enough to have several close (real) friends along the way. Once I started at SS Number 3, a small one-room schoolhouse close to my home, I found that I got on well with several of the girls. Shirley Ellis, Kathleen Clark, Jean McArter, Annie Hull, and Fern

White were early co-conspirators of mine. We were a happy bunch who enjoyed living in the area and spending time with each other. We would stay in touch for years and, for the most part, we remained close friends. Some of them—like Fern, my eventual sister-in-law— became actual family years later. Like me, these girls were free spirits, and we spent quite a lot of time together outdoors, even as young adults.

Above: I snapped this picture of Fern White, Mary Smith, Kathleen Clark, and Jean McArter, my early co-conspirators, perched on a large rock near what we called Black Bridge (now called Hoggs Bridge). We were inseparable in those days, and we remained close friends for many years.

Most of my earliest and fondest memories involve being in the outdoors. I certainly recall spending my fair share of time outside, in the mud, climbing trees, digging for skunks, swimming in the river, bouncing the ball against the barn, or generally getting into harmless mischief by endlessly exploring the world around me. Although many people in those days seemed to think little girls belonged in pretty dresses, learning about domestic responsibilities with their mothers, and planning for a future family of their own, that sugar-and-spice worldview was never one I shared. I needed to run, and nothing made me happier than when I was elbow-deep in mud and mischief.

Perhaps I inherited some of that fire from Daddy? I imagine he did more than his fair share of running around and mischief-making as a young boy on the farm in Ireland. But although I was a bit rebellious and liked to stir the pot, I was always basically content, good-natured, and carefully curious. I enjoyed an occasional prank (perhaps more occasional than some would have preferred) and some good-natured mischief, but no one ever got hurt.

I remember one time when the wife of my mother's cousin was visiting. Her name was Lizzy Button and, as seen through the eyes of a child, she struck me as a bit grouchy. This, in my mind at the time, gave me free licence to prank her.

As she was having tea at our table, focusing entirely on her conversation with my mother, I secretly tied her apron strings to the rungs of the wooden chair behind her back. Neither my mother nor her guest took note of a busy child whirring about at their feet as they sipped their tea and chatted into the afternoon—that is, until Cousin Lizzy got up to leave and was abruptly jerked back down into her chair, as she was firmly tethered in place. By that time, I had lost interest and moved on to my next pursuit, so I didn't see or hear the fallout first-hand, but I can still well remember my mother sternly demanding, "Why did you do that, Jane?" It was something she often needed to ask me.

I admit that I did do some devilish tricks in my youth, but I always took a healthy share of the blame when the dust settled. That is, unless I could talk my way clear of it, or in cases where Daddy was concerned. Perhaps I inherited my blazing spirit from Daddy, and perhaps he remembered his own fiery youth and decided to cut me slack in the punishment department, but Daddy seldom got too worked up or mad at me. I never faced the sore end of the strap, even when I might well have deserved or even needed a tuning-up.

My mother, on the other hand, would give out at me more often, but I could usually talk her down. I do remember one time when my mother was cross with me, and all my fast talk was for naught. As children do from time to time, I had acted up in public. Worse yet, I had acted up in church. While I don't entirely recall what I did to rile her, I know it made her very cross. My mother was quite certain that I had done wrong, and after hauling me out of the sanctuary, she gave me the lecture of my life.

I suspect the problem was that I did not really like church, nor did I like wearing my Sunday best. Fancy hats and white gloves, fashion necessities for churchgoing little girls in those days, cramped my more rugged style preferences. Truth be known, in my youth, I would rather have been outside the church enjoying the nice weather by puddling in a nearby stream, but I suspect that excuse hadn't held any sway with my mother on that particular morning. I don't recall getting a spanking for my transgression that day, but I sure came within a whisper of it.

Of course, none of this is to suggest that I got out of attending church each week. I even sang in the choir for a time. Being part of the church was important to my parents both as a spiritual experience and a social event. Everyone on the concession went to church and, in the end, this contributed to Daddy curtailing his own attendance.

You see, Daddy was known for his frequent appearances in the local pub, and sometimes he was the subject of whispered conversations after church. One day he caught wind of this chatter, and it didn't go over big. I don't remember Daddy attending too many Sunday services after that happened, but Tony and I were still expected to go.

As my friend Kathleen was also expected to go for services, we made the experience a weekly adventure. We would often bike to church together, which gave me a reason to enjoy Sunday mornings more than when it was a stuffy family outing. You see, I would save just enough each week from the offering plate allowance that my mother doled out to get an ice cream cone on the pedal home. This was probably not what my parents had intended for the coins they gave me, but I somehow rationalized it all in my young mind. Perhaps Bradley suggested the idea? Yeah—probably it was Bradley's suggestion.

❧

Bradley's influence aside, I have certainly always been my own person with my own mind, but I never remember feeling alone or disadvantaged in any way. My childhood was a time when I was surrounded by dear friends and family. For one, my grandmother, Mary Jane Alcock, was usually close at hand. She had been there at my birth, and as she lived with us, she was there nearly every day thereafter, until August 2, 1942, when she passed on. I even got the bedroom that she used when she was at home. The room was downstairs, off the parlour.

I was always quite proud of my simple little room, but like so many children before and since, I was eager to put my own stamp on my own room when the time came. I was only ten or twelve years old, but with my mother's help, I managed to get some wallpaper, and I redecorated. I remember that the wallpaper was covered with big and bold yellow flowers. Perhaps I was bringing some of the outside in, or maybe I did have a girly side to my personality after all. Either way, I liked it, and that was all that mattered.

The decorative paper covered the old and uneven horsehair plaster walls of the house, but not everything needed covering. In fact, the last time I went through the front door of our old farmhouse, I noticed that, just inside the front door on the plaster of the wall, it is written, "Mary and Jane Ovington papered this in 1945." It may be just a wall, but to me, this is one instance of the many wonderful and lasting memories that I have of simpler days at home on the Ovington Family Farm.

CHAPTER 4

SCHOOL DAZE

*You've got to do your own growing, no matter how
tall your grandfather was.—An Irish Proverb*

I turned 6 years old in 1938, which signalled that it was time for me to
leave behind my wild days of carefree exploration of the barn, fields,
and bush behind the farm in favour of a more regular and structured
day in class. At the time, there was not the same emphasis placed on
formal education that there is today, as chores and working at home
took far greater precedence in the minds of most parents and within the
community. Also, as girls were expected to grow into wives, the need
for higher learning was not the same as it is for my granddaughters.
Nonetheless, primary education was still an important part of everyday
life for most young people between the ages of 6 and 14, and passing
grades were the expectation of most parents, in addition to the on-farm
responsibilities most children had.

In rural Ontario in the 1930s, primary learning consisted of core
subjects like reading, writing, math, and history, all of which were
typically delivered by one or two dedicated teachers in one-room
schoolhouses scattered throughout the province. My educational career
started (and eventually ended) at the small yellow-brick-clad School
Section (SS) Number 3 (Morris Township), located about a mile from
my house. The building was simple, boasted no hydro or running
water, and offered amenities like twin outhouses (one for the boys and

one for the girls), a wood-fired stove for the winter, and a large water pail with a wooden dipper at the back of the room should anyone need a drink of water during the day. It did the trick but couldn't hold a candle to the schools of today.

The notion of going to school is not one that I ever remember loving or hating one way or the other. I am not sure I ever thought about it. It was just the way things were, I suppose. I was never a great or aspiring scholar, but I was good enough to get by, and when I worked at it, my marks were never terrible.

To be honest, I think my biggest problem with school was more motivational than it was academic. While I enjoyed school events like baseball, sleigh rides, school festivals, Christmas concerts, and all the other fun stuff (stuff that never appeared on any of the tests), I liked other things far more. I enjoyed the freedom of activities like hunting with my brother, mastering the wooden stilts Daddy had made for us, swinging from our gnarled old apple tree at home, splashing about in the river, or helping Daddy in the barn, so school was not high on my list of priorities. Of course, Daddy and my mother rightly insisted that both Tony and I receive an education, so when the time came, off I trotted to class and on to my first real foray into the world beyond our own farm gate.

Above: SS No. 3 (Morris)—the place where my school career began and ended. Also, this is where many of my lifelong friendships first took root.

As each stand-alone school zone was just a few square miles in size, there were no centralized school buses or coordinated transportation system like schools have today. This meant that most of the children walked to and from their closest school regardless of weather. Rain or shine, I either walked or rode my old bike to school each weekday, arriving before the bell, which rang out sharply at 8:30 a.m. In the cold winter months, when the snow was piled high, it was not uncommon for me to strap on the clunky old wooden skis that Daddy had made. In addition to being a fun ride, skiing to school seemed to shorten the trek and add to the adventure.

Regardless of how we did it, it was our job to get to school on time, so as I recall, Daddy never drove us (he saw that as interfering with our responsibilities). Sometimes, neighbours passing by our gate, with their own children in tow, would take pity on us and give Tony and me a ride. This was a rarity, but it was especially appreciated when the weather was bitterly cold, blustery, particularly wet, or otherwise just too miserable for easy walking.

Rain and snow aside, the daily trek wasn't too much of a burden except for during the thaw. It was at this point each spring that Tony and I had an added complication when it came to getting to school ahead of the bell each morning. This is because the Maitland River cut through our farm between our house and the gravel road near the laneway. During a winter thaw, or in the spring when the water was up over the bridge and we couldn't get out by foot, horse, or vehicle, we had to go the long way around through the muddy fields. On occasion, we would try to cross the fast-flowing or ice-crusted river, but that was not something that Daddy or my mother ever encouraged. The Maitland was often fast and cold, and it would have been easy for a wee one like me to get swept away.

I had more than one close call with the torrent. On one such occasion, as I was attempting a crossing, the ice gave way under my feet. Fortunately, just as I broke through and dropped toward the water, Tony snapped me up by the back of my jacket. I was none the worse for wear save for wet feet, but I had learned my lesson (for a while at least).

Fate was on my side that time, but Bruno, my short-haired little hound, was not so lucky. One spring afternoon, when the waters were especially high, Bruno and I were trailing behind Daddy as he waded across the bridge in his hip-boots. Bruno, who had run ahead of me, was swept off the bridge by the surge of the roaring river. For some reason, Daddy turned and caught sight of us. With a thundering roar, Daddy ordered me back. I froze safely in place, but it was too late for little Bruno. He fought the current, but he was just too weak to make it back to the riverbank past the swirl of the seven boilers. That was a terribly sad day, but it offered a permanent reminder of how risky the riverbank could be.

In the summer, that same river was much less daunting an obstacle, and it served as a refreshing bathtub for lots of local people. In fact, we never had a bathtub in that house, which makes sense, as we didn't have running water or hydro either. In the winter, we would be expected to bathe once per week in a laundry tub beside the box stove in the living room. We had to draw our water, by pail, from the soft-water cistern located in a small room off the kitchen. My mother would heat the water on the stove and, because heating enough water for a full bath was quite a big job, Tony and I had to share. As you might expect, I always liked to bathe first.

Summer was quite a different matter. We put the washtub away for the season because we had our own river nearby. I would just take a bar of soap and clean up there. That river functioned as our washtub, swimming pool, fishing hole, and, when the water was high, barrier to the outside world. Years later, my husband Clarence would joke that he went through hell and "crossed high water" to get to me. He might have been right, but I think it was worth it when you consider the prize he found on the riverbank (me).

Spring thaw and summer baths notwithstanding, SS No. 3 was where I spent much of my time in those days, and as I have already said, I was not always at the top of my grade. I remember that I particularly disliked history class. There was just something about studying old men that have been dead for years, who explored or invented something that I had never seen, that was of absolutely no interest to me. Perhaps I was just young, but at the time I couldn't imagine that I would ever need to know the subject matter for a future job. To make matters worse, I didn't find it interesting in any way, shape, or form, so I checked out. I made it through history class, but let's just say that I did better in my other subjects.

Bookwork aside, I got along with most of my classmates most of the time, but there may have been an occasional tussle with the neighbour boys. I know now that it was my own fault for taking their bait, but in my younger days, that was hard to see and even harder to resist. There was no denying that I was a scrappy wee thing who could give as well (or better) as I got.

Some of the other kids liked to rev me up, and in those days, you needed to stand up for yourself. If that meant an occasional punch-up, then so be it. I was all too prepared to do what I had to do, and my attitude made me a target for some. Usually, it was all harmless fun and tomfoolery, like the time an older boy hit me with his geography book. He was just stirring the pot, but I didn't care. I reacted quickly, and I took him out. We might have laughed that one off, but other times, the taunting was something else entirely.

Most of the houses with telephones on our concession road were connected by a party-line system. You don't see this system much today, but in the past, they were often used in areas with smaller or more spread-out populations. A party line meant that we all shared a single telephone line, but each house had its own telephone and receiver. Only one house could make or receive a call at any one time, but once the line was activated and a call was taking place, anyone with a telephone on the line could listen in on conversations being had by anyone else on the line. The community was already small, so, as you can imagine, this telephone system made keeping secrets next to impossible.

Because of this, the fact that Daddy spent time in the local pub was one of the worst-kept secrets in the community. Everyone knew when he called home from the pub. Everyone knew that the horses would eagerly find their own way home after they were made to stand waiting for Daddy to finish one more last drink with his pals. And everyone knew that, on the occasions when my mother and I would stand on the front stoop and listen carefully for the distinctive sound of the bells on the team's harnesses as they got louder and louder, coming closer and closer, that Daddy was on his way home and would need help unhitching the team and getting into the house (the team knew its own way home and often made the trip while Daddy slept one off on the wagon).

On a clear night, you could hear the team as they headed out of Brussels almost as clearly as you could hear lips set aflutter with gossip up and down the line. My classmates would hear the news as their parents whispered about the Ovingtons, and when they dared to mention the happenings to me at school the next day, a flare-up was sure to follow. I loved Daddy, and I was always quick and fierce to defend him when they called him the "wild Irishman." Like lots of people in those days, he took a drink, but he also worked hard—and despite his temper, he was never nasty to me.

Occasional scuffles aside, a lot of hellery went on at SS No. 3, and somehow, I found myself in the middle of quite a lot of it. Like the time I grabbed a young lad's boots when he was skating because he had said nasty things about Daddy. I am not sure how he walked home that day in the snow without his boots, but he chose his words more carefully after that. There was also the time when someone threw a handful of bullets into the wood-fired stove in the schoolhouse. As I remember it, the plan was simple. Mrs. Dyer, a teacher who was not terribly well liked by many of the students, had a habit of standing directly on top of the heat grate to keep warm during the coldest and most frosty days of winter. The school was never very warm in the winter, and the kids seemed to think she was sucking up all the heat for herself, so a few decided to take matters into their own hands. I can honestly say that I was not at all responsible for that incident, but I am not sure everyone was entirely convinced of my innocence.

Notwithstanding my scrappy way, I was blessed with some tremendously good friends. We spent loads of time, both at school during the week and in and around each other's homes and farms on weekends, getting to know each other. We did lots of silly but harmless things in our spare time, and even during times when we were supposed to be doing something far more productive. I remember when it was decided to dig out some skunks on the walk to school. I am not sure what we were thinking when we decided to do that, but I do remember deciding.

One warm spring morning on our walk through the ploughed field toward school, we caught sight of some tracks around a hole. Tony sprinted home to get a shovel, because this was clearly more important than our classes. It took a lot of work and time, but we were rewarded for our troubles with three big fat skunks. I am sure that my mother smelled us coming long before she saw the black and white fur of our quarry, and she was less than impressed (I wonder why). As she prepared to give out at us for skipping class without permission, we argued our case. Even she had to admit that the money we would get from our haul would be nice.

By the time we finished scraping and stretching those hides, we must have been a ripe, smelly mess. I guess it was probably good that bathing in the river was the thing to do in those days. I am sure my mother would not have wanted me anywhere near the house after that ordeal.

There was also the time when Annie Hull and I were out and about on a Saturday. I don't recall what we were up to, but we had been gone all day and failed to check in with our parents until Annie went home for lunch. Rather than go home myself, I decided to sit quietly in the window-well at Annie's house. She brought me out a tea biscuit when she was done with her meal and then let me know that Daddy and most of the neighbourhood were hunting through the fields and down by the river looking for me. This caused quite a stir, as everyone thought that I was lost, or worse, when in fact we were just hanging out. I came perilously close to the strap that day.

But I was no stranger to mischief, nor to the fallout it sometimes caused. I recall a time when, after Grandma Alcock died, my mother's cousin and that cousin's grandson came to visit for a few days. My mother's cousin struck my young brain as a crabby old coot, so I decided to make her stay less than comfortable. In hindsight, I am not proud of this behaviour, but I went to the river and captured a crayfish (we called them *crabs*) in an old red hankie. Somehow, that critter quietly found its way under the covers of her bed. I can still hear her frantically screaming when she found what I had left for her.

When the screaming finally subsided, I simply asked if our guests were going home soon. As was to be expected, that comment triggered some consequences. My mother gave out at me for that one. Or perhaps mother was just upset when she and Daddy found another crayfish in their own bed? My memory is a bit fuzzy on that detail, so who's to say what happened?

But my friends and I were not just into mischief. We certainly enjoyed pranks and jokes, but we enjoyed lots of things. Mostly we just liked spending time together (my grandchildren call this *hanging out*).

Like the time when some of the neighbourhood boys, Jean McArter, and I went pigeon-hunting. Jean was a great friend even though she was younger than me. Her brother Bill was a classmate of mine, so I guess that is how we first met.

In any event, Jean and I went along with the boys when they decided to hunt up a bunch of pigeons to pass the time on a weekend. We were successful, and with a quarry that was not to be wasted. The next day, Jean's mother, Nellie, made all of us a feast of fresh-baked pigeon pie. You know, you haven't lived until you have enjoyed a piece of pigeon pie. At the time, wasting the meat would have been entirely unthinkable, but I suspect mothers today would be far less enthusiastic with the notion of preparing and serving fresh pigeon pie to guests.

Above: Me and some of my school pals at SS No. 3, including (left to right) Annie Hull, Kathleen Clark, Jane Ovington (me), Bill McArter, Shirley Ellis, Ellen Draper, and Fern White (my future husband's sister).

Whether in school or after class, my time at SS No. 3 was memorable to say the least, and most of those memories are wrapped fondly around the people I met there.

In addition to my good friends, I also liked my teachers. One teacher in particular went above and beyond to help me. During what was to be my grade 8 year, there was a late snow melt and a lot of spring rain and runoff. This caused the river near my house to crest well over the banks, flooding area creeks and causing me to miss a lot of school because I couldn't safely leave the property. At the time, I figured I had learned just about everything I needed to know to get by in life, so I decided to call it quits. My school days were behind me, and like Daddy when he was my age, I turned my attention to the world of work. But regardless of my plans, my teacher had other ideas.

One day when I was in town, I met up with Mr. Ziggler. He wanted to know where I had been and when he could expect me back. I told him that I was not planning to return to school, but this strategy was not something he was willing to accept. Perhaps he saw something in me and was determined to help me, even if I didn't yet know that I needed his help. Mr. Ziggler chatted up my mother and convinced her that I belonged in his class. At the very least, he wanted me to finish grade 8. It was probably an easy argument to advance, because my mother wanted me to become a nurse, something that would require additional schooling to achieve.

My concern was the entrance exam. Now that I had left school, I needed to pass a test to get back in at my own grade level. Mr. Ziggler promised that he would work with me and assured me that, with work and effort, I would pass the entrance exam. And he was true to his word. He dedicated his time with me at recess, during the noon-hour break, and even after class, for weeks. Some days I wondered why I would come back and if it would all be worth it in the end.

Above: The crew at SS No. 3 (Morris) in 1946. Back row—Bill McArter, Jean McArter, Ellen Draper, Annie Hull, Bill Ziggler (teacher), Jane Ovington (me), Fern White, Shirley Ellis, and Mary Smith. Middle row—Archie Hull, Lorne Draper, George Hislop, Marion Hull, Mildred Marks, Shirley Hislop, Edith Marks, Evelyn Hislop, and Shirley Jameson. Front row—Ross White, Stuart Smith, Ken White, Charles Hull, Bob Jameson, Bill Jameson, and Gordon Clark.

Eventually, the hard work paid off. I passed the exam and graduated grade 8, and I owe it all to Mr. Ziggler. Other than my parents and family, Mr. Ziggler was one of the first people to believe in me—even before I believed in myself. I will always appreciate his help and support.

❧

While all of this was happening, my young life outside of school continued to unfold. That was where the real fun stuff happened. After class ended for the day, I always had little jobs to do at home. In addition to dusting all the flat surfaces in the house each Saturday morning and filling the wood-box each day from the woodshed out back, I brought the cows up from the bush or the flats, wherever they were grazing that day, so they could be milked and fed.

As I got older, at the ripe old age of 12, I needed to do more around the farm, so I helped by milking cows. I was always given the strippers, the hardest part of the job, but I usually didn't complain. We only had about a dozen cows, but that kept us busy, and it kept us in fresh milk and cream. You would think that the cattle would also keep us in beef, but that was not the case. I guess you can only eat cows once, but you can milk them for years.

Instead of beef, I ate a lot of peanut butter sandwiches in my youth, especially for lunch at school. You can't take peanut butter to school these days, but allergies just weren't a thing you heard about back then. I'm not sure why. Beef products were expensive. Steak was unheard of, but we did have hamburger sometimes.

Once in a while, we would have a pig butchered. It was done in the yard. I hated when that happened, and I would usually hide whenever the actual butchering was being done. After the terrible deed was over, Daddy and my mother would spend several days making head cheese, making sausages, and curing the meat. My mother would also make her own laundry soap, but it wasn't until some time later that I learned of the ingredients needed for that.

My mother would use the milk and cream from the cows in her cooking and baking, and on special occasions, she was known to make homemade chocolate syrup so we could enjoy a big glass of cold chocolate milk. Chocolate milk was always one of my favourite things, even when I grew older (that and Jell-O). Times may have been tough, but our meals were as hardy as they were tasty.

Funny, but while everything at home was patched, rigged up, or mended in some way, our butter churn was the only new item that I ever remember having at home. My mother loved her churn. We all took turns on the handle. It sure made for good buttermilk. Looking back, I guess fresh butter was just too important to risk a broken churn.

But housework made up only part of our days. There was always more to be done outside and in the barn. In the winter, we pulled hay from the mow before it got dark. This dusty job had to be done early because there was no hydro, and the hay was needed for the feeding each night. We had coal-oil lanterns for the other chores, but Daddy didn't allow me to take a lantern into the hay-mow, for good reason.

While there were always odd jobs and things to do around the farm, we were never short of help. Daddy was always taking people in. Drifters who were moving from place to place looking for a good meal and a warm bed in return for a day's work often found a place with us. A man by the name of Johnston Kerns was with us for a while. He was a nice man, but he was a bit of a drinker. He hid a bottle in the pump house until my mother found it one day, and then she fixed him. She dumped the whole bottle onto the dirt floor. I don't expect he was too impressed, but I think he found a new hiding place for his bottle after that.

I'm sad to say that I often played tricks on Johnston. One time I pinched him, after which he gave a quick chase, but I was saved by my mother. Despite my troublemaking ways, he called me Janey, and we got on quite well most of the time. Unfortunately, he and my brother, Tony, couldn't make the same claim. They were like oil and water … mixed with fire. One night at the supper table, as a consequence of my clowning, Tony and Johnston got into it in a serious way. Johnston left later that same night, and I never saw him again. I wonder what ever became of him.

After Johnston left, Daddy had a hired man named Jack. He was a bit awkward, but a kinder man was never to be found. And he was a good worker. I remember that he rolled his own cigarettes, and that Daddy disliked those who rolled their own cigarettes. I am not sure why he felt this way. It was not that Daddy disliked smokers or even tobacco in general. He smoked a pipe and took an occasional chew. But for some reason, rolling cigarettes crossed a line for him.

He also thought that it was totally inappropriate for a woman to smoke, but it was fine if women took a drink. Daddy could be funny that way, but despite the bad habit, Jack was with us for a while. I was glad for this, because as long as he was, I was freed up to spend time on more leisurely activities with my friends.

In those days, we liked to hang out at Alf and Millie Nichol's place. We would chat, play music, and even help them with chores and odd jobs around the house when they needed it. It was just a casual place that we all enjoyed. My cousin Jim would saw away on the violin as Alf played the piano, while the rest of us would play cards. Canasta, euchre, and pinochle were favourite ways to pass the time. Alf and Millie never had children of their own, but they always had kids at the house. Our gang of friends had a lot of good times at Alf and Millie's. They were truly hospitable and wonderful people who I remained friends with until Millie passed away, followed by Alf, in May of 2010.

When we were looking for something that was less casual than a hangout or a card game, we would often find our way to the latest picture show in Wingham. Wingham was a small community just thirteen miles west of Brussels, so we didn't have to go far from home. We weren't fussy, but our group really liked watching some of the movies featuring Roy Rogers, his faithful horse trigger, his friend Dale Evans, and his dog Bullet. These movies were quite popular because they were action-packed, and for the time, the special effects were amazing. I guess teenagers in my day were not that different from teenagers today.

If the show wasn't on or if it wasn't appealing to us, there was always a dance, ball game, or hockey games in Brussels. We lived in a great neighbourhood and, in those days, nearly any neighbour would give us a ride into town on a Saturday night. It was just what you did. I am not sure why, but everyone seemed to go to town each Saturday night, except for my own family. But that didn't stop me. Sometimes, we would take our horse Pete and the cutter to the hockey games. We would park at the church shed and then meet up with friends to watch the game.

As time marched on, our gang came to include Clarence White; his sister, Fern; Tony; and me. This was all before Clarence and I were married or even formally dating, for that matter. We were just teenagers, and according to my very protective Daddy, I was far too young to date any boy. While Clarence was a nice young man, he was still a young man, and Daddy would simply not allow me to go out with him. At least that is what my mother told me. So, for now, we were just friends, and we all enjoyed spending time together.

But Clarence was the only boyfriend I ever had, and even if I didn't know for sure at the time, others clearly saw that we had eyes for each other. In 1996, Elwin Hall, one of my teachers from SS No. 3, wrote a poem entitled *An Ode to SS #3 (Morris)*. His comments about me and my old classmates made me laugh. The poem read:

> I thought I'd like to write a rhyme
> About the kids that I have taught.
> I may not mention all your names
> 'Cause my memory is not so hot.
> Some names will bring sad memories
> Of people that have died.
> Let's think of them most kindly
> And remember them with pride.
>
> When I went to your little school
> In 1943,
> Jerry was the biggest boy,
> But not as big as me.
>
> Frank Alcock was extremely sharp,
> At math he was the best,
> But Cousin Kathleen kept right up
> And put him to the test.
>
> The Hulls had kids in every class,
> With Archie, Charles, and Bill,
> Marian, and Annie,
> They helped the school to fill.
> Shirley Ellis off the fourth,
> How could one be so thin?

A lot of water o'er the dam
Has passed along since then.

And little Janey Ovington,
Now what a pretty sight.
She had one aim right from the start:
She was determined to be a White.

And then there were McArters,
There was Billy, Don, and Jean,
With parents Nell and Ivan,
No finer family seen.

The Smiths lived over on the Sixth,
There was Shirley and her brother,
The father's name was Ernie,
I've forgotten the name of the mother.
And then there were the Armstrongs,
There was Lloyd and sister May,
The father bought an Edsel,
That was a happy day.

The Charlie Drapers had two kids,
There was Ellen and wee Lorne,
They were a happy pair of kids,
They smiled at me each morn.
The Marx girls came each day to school,
To me they looked alike,
Their father was a joker,
'Twas Halloween each night.

I near forgot the Hyslops,
There was Evelyn, Florence, and George,
And one more name I have forgot,
My mind has hit a gorge.

And Gordon Clark came from the west,
Of Gramps he liked to talk,
So with the Hulls he went on home,
Together they would walk.

Nor Fern and Ross came every day,
Their name of course was White,
And after school at 4 o'clock,
They went back home each night.
I guess I've nearly mentioned
All the kids that came to me,
And in my memory so clear,
I still can plainly see.

This special day is very special,
Especially for me.
It brings back many memories,
From good old number three.
I hope that we can meet again,
To talk about the past.
Let's meet again in 3 years hence,
For time is going fast.

So here's a toast to Number 3,
To scholars from the past,
Good friends to me you'll always be,
As long as life shall last.

Perhaps my marriage to Clarence was always in the cards, but at least in those early days, my group of friends enjoyed spending time together before the world crept in and complicated things.

Chapter 5

Onward Toward Tomorrow

The trick is growing up without growing old.—*Denis Waitley*

As a teenager, I always cried the blues about wanting to make my own spending money. My days on the farm gave me a good work ethic, so I wasn't afraid of hard work, but in those days, there were only so many jobs that girls were allowed to do. Most of the outside physical work was reserved for the boys and young men. As was to be expected of a young girl, domestic work was high on that list of "appropriate jobs," but for me, that was just not what I had in mind for my first steps into the world of work.

I'm not entirely sure what I was looking for. Maybe everyone wants to start a step or two up the ladder? In my younger years, I did some babysitting and odd jobs around the neighbourhood, but I didn't stray too far from home. That was until the summer of 1948.

My first real job was an eight-week stint working for Libby's, a food cannery in Chatham, in southern Ontario. Working in the agricultural harvest has always been grueling—so much so that today, many Canadian youth simply won't do it, so the sector relies heavily on foreign workers to get the crops off and in on time. This is particularly true for tobacco, tender fruit, and certain vegetables like cucumbers and tomatoes. While foreign workers were still used in the summer of 1948, the agricultural harvest and further processing of the picked produce was an industry where young people from Canada could make good money, assuming they were prepared to work like they had never worked before.

My adventure at Libby's started one afternoon when Daddy returned home from a visit with Mr. Thompson. Daddy sometimes made the trip to the Thompsons' farm because Mr. Thompson was so well known for the special cider he would ferment in his basement that the locals called him Cider Bill. At the time, there were lots of people in the area who made their own variety of home-brew for private sale, but I guess Daddy had a fondness for Cider Bill's recipe.

Mr. Thompson had a teenage daughter named Bernice who was a bit older than me. While Bernice and I had not been friends previously—in fact, we had never met before—Daddy thought it would be a good idea if I made the trip to Chatham with Bernice for the upcoming tomato season. He returned from Cider Bill's one afternoon and declared that, since I was always complaining about wanting a job, I should plan on heading south to work in the cannery with Bernice. I suppose Daddy was just happy to have me travel with someone from the neighbourhood rather than alone (he never would have permitted me to make the trip alone), and I was happy for a shot at a little independence.

Bernice was a veteran of the cannery. She has taken a similar job the summer prior, so she already knew the lay of the land. At Daddy's urging, Bernice and I met up, discussed the idea, and committed to working for six to eight weeks during the tomato season to make some pocket money. It was going to be hard work, but we decided it would be worth it.

The demand for workers was such that you could just show up at the cannery door and get work, so there was no need to make arrangements or to interview in advance. Bernice and I simply packed our bags, hopped on a bus at Belgrave, and headed south. We made the 140-mile trip to Chatham in just a few short hours. This was the farthest I had ever been from home, and I don't mind saying that I was scared and very concerned about the prospect of being alone and so far from my parents. I might have been a scrappy loner, but the bus station in London where we had to transfer, and the streets of Chatham once we arrived, looked quite different from the farm fields of Morris Township.

Fortunately, Bernice and I were to be billeted in the same house, with the McDougalls, a Salvation Army family. The house had two double beds in two different rooms, so Bernice and I were joined in the house by two other young girls, Hazel Juntzie and Phyllis Schultz, who we'd met on the bus into Chatham. They were Mennonite ladies and probably as apprehensive as I was about being alone and so far from home. They were nice people, and the four of us got on quite well from the start.

Despite the pleasantness of our surroundings, our careful plans were not to be. Bernice ended up going home early after she discovered that the special young man she had encountered the previous summer, and who was most probably the reason for her interest in a return to the cannery, had moved along to other fair interests. She was scorned and almost immediately lost interest in the job and any cash it promised. Hazel and Phyllis also went home early. Never one to quit, I was the only one of the four left to stay long enough to finish what we had all started.

I worked daily on the tomato line, where I was required to quickly snatch up any rotten or wormy fruit that came rolling down the conveyor so it didn't get into the product lines. I tossed all the rotten, worm-infested, or over-ripe tomatoes into a special metre that would divert them from getting into the stewing vats or tomato juice. This castoff was monitored closely by management and used as a gauge of our individual productivity. But despite our best efforts, inevitably some bad fruit and bugs got past us. After seeing the process in action, to this day, I still wince a little when I drink tomato juice.

The whole process was messy work, and not the kind of job that one would like to be doing after a heavy night out on the town. Fortunately, as I was more of a homebody, that was not something I had to worry very much about. Many of my coworkers, however, could not make the same claim. Often young workers, looking for their first taste of freedom, would show up at work for a few shifts, collect some cash, and then vanish after a day or two on the line. The work was not for everyone, but as I was no stranger to hard work, I rolled up my sleeves and dug in up to my elbows.

The transient nature of the workforce meant that I worked with new people almost every day, but I do remember one lady who was always around. Her name was Ta'Mikel Ziki, and she was a regular on the downstairs line. I remember that she wore a new clean white blouse after every break. Whenever I worked with her on the downstairs line, we needed to lift two full tomato cans at a time, one in each hand, out of steaming-hot vats as they moved along the line. We would then place the hot cans gently on the conveyor for the next stage in the process.

While we were glad to have heavy gloves to wear when we did this, it was hard hot work, and by the end of a long shift, your hands were so black, tired, and throbbing that you couldn't even straighten your fingers, let alone wash your hands clean. Today I suffer from terrible arthritis in my hands and fingers, and I often wonder if my time working with Ta'Mikel is the culprit for some of my pain today.

But Chatham wasn't all hard work and drudgery, and I was very lucky to be living with the McDougall family. They made my time in southern Ontario fun and memorable. We were supposed to do our own laundry, but Mrs. McDougall told me to set mine out, and she took care of it with the family laundry. She really was a kind person. In return, I helped dry the dinner dishes each night and did other odd jobs around the house to pitch in. Mr. McDougall—his first name was Lorne, but I was raised that you would never refer to elders informally or by their first name—would wake me up each day and make me a wonderful breakfast of hot tea and peanut butter on toast. He also packed me a bag lunch, which I augmented each day by purchasing chocolate milk as my one vice. That menu took me back to the boxed lunches and homemade chocolate syrup that my mother would send with me to SS No. 3.

When breakfast was done, Mr. McDougall would walk me to the corner, where we would both catch our bus to work. He also worked at the cannery, so I had a travelling companion each morning and night. Chatham somehow felt like the big city to me, so I was glad for the guidance and for the company. I had been so isolated in Huron County, and my time in Chatham opened my eyes to new people, sights, and sounds.

For example, that was the first time I had ever encountered people from parts of the world other than places like Ireland. In many ways, that summer was a bit of a cultural awakening for me. It was also a time when my relationship with Clarence and my other friends continued to grow. I remember one time when Clarence, his friend Don McArter, and my friend Dorothy made the trip by car to visit me. The boys slept in Clarence's Mercury, but Mrs. McDougall said it was okay for me to invite my girlfriend to sleep on the couch. Our group spent the next day catching up and exploring the area by car. We didn't have much money, but we felt like we had the world by the tail.

Clarence, perhaps signalling his growing interest in me, bought me a wonderful basket of fresh local peaches. Fresh peaches have a wonderful smell. He knew that I loved peaches, and I was so happy to receive the gift. Fresh fruit was expensive, so we didn't get it every day. I remember that they tasted like candy. I ate two or three of them myself and then gave the rest to Mrs. McDougall for use in her kitchen.

A day or so later, when I returned from work for the evening meal, I found a small nappy at every place around the table heaped evenly with fresh sweet diced peaches. Everyone enjoyed the special treat, including the McDougalls' young daughter, Merlyn, who I was quite fond of.

Above: At just 16 years old, I stand on the lawn of the McDougall home in Chatham with the family's young daughter, Merlyn.

A short time after Clarence's visit, my time in Chatham ended, and I returned home. But before I left, Mrs. McDougall took me shopping. After all, how could I go home after a summer of hard work without some special purchases from the local stores and a final meal of bologna and sliced tomatoes at the local Salvation Army Church? Somehow that made the long bus ride home alone seem more bearable. I can't imagine how I survived the transfer in London myself, but I did it. Clarence showed up at the bus station to drive me home, and that was the last of the cannery for me. I was home at last, and my mother was so happy when she saw the beautiful new coat, boots, and other purchases from my shopping excursion.

This was to be my last full year as a child living at home, so I wanted to make the most of it. Yet the lure of a job again pulled me in. Not long after I arrived home from Chatham, I learned of another income opportunity—only this time, it was much closer to home. The Queen's Hotel was and is still located in Blyth, a small community just 13 miles south-west of Brussels. They were bringing the hydro lines through the area that year, and the hotel was home to twenty-two hydro workers, including five year-round regulars. Hotel owners Grover Clair and his wife needed a live-in housekeeper, and the job offered a paycheque of twelve dollars per week, which I saw as very reasonable pay. I was eager to get out into the world, so I took the job for a couple of months before Christmas that year. I boarded full-time with the owners and learned the ropes before returning home for Christmas of 1948.

In those days, we didn't travel far from home due to costs and the fact that we had daily chores and animals to tend, but we still liked to "get away" for the holidays and on special occasions. For our family, we often spent time at the home of Uncle Dick and Aunt Jean. In fact, Uncle Dick's farm was where our family usually spent Christmas Day. As I think about it, we probably went to Uncle Dick's for Christmas because my parents hosted a roast goose dinner for the Alcock family each year on New Year's Day.

Above: We didn't get away from home much because of chores and the cost of travel, so family togetherness was important. My cousin Mary Bernard and I were great friends. Here we pose for a snap together.

My mother always raised her own meat geese, and she prepared the most plump and delicious one for the first meal of each year. In fact, that seemed to be what we always had for our most special meals. I had never even tasted turkey until I had it one year at Clarence's parents' house. I liked it very much, but roast goose still takes me back to my mother's table, even though it is far rarer as a holiday meal than turkey is these days.

Much like we did following our New Year's meal, after our Christmas dinner, festivities continued throughout the day. Daddy and the other adults would enjoy a wee nip of whiskey (or two). We would take a ride on the sleigh or listen and sing along to some old records. Christmas in those days was far less about gifts and far more about group activities and togetherness than it is today. Even still, I can't and won't claim that gifts were entirely foreign to us. After all, what kid doesn't want presents at Christmas? I always got something wonderful.

As a child, I remember eagerly waiting for a special box to arrive in the mail each year from some Irish friends of the family. The box usually contained colouring books, crayons, horns, whistles, and some candy canes for Tony and me. It was certainly a holiday highlight in those early years. When it finally came, we had it made. If I remember right, my mother typically sent the same friends one of the geese she had raised, on the train, as a Christmas gift. They reciprocated with a box of goodies for us. It was a good arrangement as far as I could tell. It certainly brightened our holiday season. Christmas was always a time with lots of family and friends around, but there was always room for one more at our table.

❦

As 1948 ended and 1949 began, I was called back to the Queen's Hotel. I started in January, and this time, in addition to the twelve dollars weekly wage, I was offered room and board, which meant I could move out of my parents' house for an extended period. It was freedom on a whole new level. The Bucks ran the dining room, so I didn't get involved in that. In a way, it was too bad, because I had trained under the tutelage of my mother, who grew everything, cooked and baked everything, mended everything, and generally ran our household like a well-oiled machine. While far from an expert, after years of coaching from her, I had at least the basic skills to help run a proper kitchen.

Instead, I was responsible for washing laundry with the old ringer washing machine, folding towels endlessly, changing bedding, and ensuring that the men had lots of hot water and towels to wash up with when they arrived home hungry after work. The men were good to me, and I enjoyed the work. For the most part, all they wanted was warm water, a clean towel to wash up with, and a hearty hot meal before bed.

It was always a bit of a scramble when the men returned in the evenings. No matter how many towels I had cleaned and had ready for them, it didn't change the fact that there was only one full bathroom on the second floor of the hotel. Aside from that, some of the rooms had running water and a small sink for washing, but that did little to stem the wash line at mealtime. When you think back, it is hard to image how everyone managed with such simple amenities. You would certainly never get along that way today.

Modest facilities aside, some of the regulars treated me like a daughter, and for the most part, we stayed friends. I left the hotel in November of 1949, but I certainly have lots of good memories from my time working there. While my memories of working at the hotel are not unpleasant, I also remember the summer of 1949 with fondness for many other reasons.

Above: Clarence and his '47 Mercury, parked in the lane by our house on the 5th Line of Morris Township. He loved that big old car.

I finally had some money in my pocket because of my tenure in both Blyth and Chatham, and some good friends by my side, so I was looking for some fun and adventure. I guess that made me a normal teenager.

I don't remember all the details, but in our quest for adventure, four of us girls rented the Argyle cottages in Goderich that summer. We had a great time together, getting a taste of our future independence. We walked barefoot in the sand on the beach, splashed in the cool clear waters of Lake Huron, and filled our days with simple fun and enjoyment. I loved the beach then, and I still love it today. It was nice to be out together, even if only for a short time.

We didn't have money to eat out all the time, like many do these days, so we made our own simple meals in our temporary basement home (the cottages). Wieners and beans were a staple, but I would be lying if I didn't admit to an occasional splurge on an ice cream cone. It wasn't fancy, but it was probably one of the most enjoyable summers that I remember in my youth. It was also my last summer as a single girl.

Above: Me and the girls at the Argyle cottage during the summer of 1949. We had fun that summer, but it was to be my last full summer of freedom before setting up a home of my own.

With the summer of the Argyle cottages behind me, Clarence proposed, and we were married at St. Paul's Anglican Church in Listowel on November 19, 1949. I now had responsibilities for a home and a man of my own. My time working at the Queen's Hotel had passed, and I quietly moved from the summer of my youth to the next stage in my young life.

CHAPTER 6

MY HOME AWAY FROM HOME

*You can't kiss an Irish girl unexpectedly. You can only kiss her
sooner than she thought you would.—An Old Irish Saying*

Clarence White and I never really dated in the way that people did
in those days—or these days, for that matter. Ours was a lengthy and
evolving courtship that happened gradually and spanned many years.
We started as acquaintances (friends of friends), then became good
friends who enjoyed spending time with each other as part of our
group, and finally, we became a couple. We had both attended SS No.
3 (Morris), our families lived only a few miles apart on the same road,
and we had common friends and connections, so our paths just seemed
to be permanently intertwined from the start.

In the years before we were married, our group of friends frequently
went back and forth from a lazy Saturday cooling off in the river near
my house or card games with friends to cutter rides before a hockey
game and ice cream cones in Brussels. Clarence was almost always part
of my life. As a young girl, I spent a lot of time at the White house
because Clarence's sister, Fern, and I were good friends. I would often
stay over with Fern, or she would stay at my place, so Clarence was no
stranger to me, or to my parents, even in those early days.

As the years passed, Clarence was just one of the group. He always
seemed to be around. He was nearly six years older than me, but we
enjoyed doing the same things, and we had a lot in common. He also

had a car (eventually), which was a nice perk when we wanted to go to a show, a hockey game, or even to the township hall for a community dance.

Clarence was even the one who taught me how to drive. I was only 16 years old when I got my driver's licence, but I practiced my driving with Clarence well before that. I was glad to have the extra freedom and the ability to move about, especially when I eventually had access to a car of my own.

I am not sure when I actually fell for Clarence, but I do remember getting a nice valentine from him after I first started school. I was quite excited to get it, and I kept it for many years after. It had a cartoon boat on it that said, "I Luv U." One time, many years after I had tucked it away for safekeeping, I mentioned it to him. He smiled in that way he often did and then claimed that he had given one to all the kids in the class. I guess you could say that burst my bubble—until I realized that perhaps he was more smitten than he cared to admit.

I don't remember our actual first date, but the first time we went out alone, just the two of us, was to a picture show. While I don't remember exactly what we did on our date, I am almost positive we would have gone to Wingham to see the latest Roy Rogers feature. That was just what young couples did at the time, and besides, Clarence and I both loved to watch Roy Rogers; his horse, Trigger; his friend Dale Evans; and his dog Bullet. These western movies were fast-paced and always interesting, and going to a show meant that we could spend time together (and maybe even hold hands).

As I got a bit older, we used to have a great time dancing at the old township hall, a mile or so up the road from where we each lived. As was the custom at the time, families, young and old, gathered there for a good time. Sometimes there were box socials, where the ladies provided a fancy and complete boxed meal for two. The boys had to bid on a meal; if successful, they would be permitted to share that dinner for two with whoever packed the box. It was supposed to be a secret, but when a young man was sweet on a girl, he usually tried pretty hard to find out which box was prepared by which girl so he could be sure to purchase the right one. I don't know if or what Clarence had to do to find out which box I brought, but I do remember sharing an occasional meal. He was always quite crafty, so I am sure he had his sources.

We didn't have much by way of extras in those days, but there was always something in the community to do. Whenever there was a dance at the township hall, everyone would come and listen to the live music. We danced across the rough old wood floor even when the knotholes made being graceful a challenge. We didn't seem to care about such things. I guess we were more focused on having fun.

That is not to say that we ignored all of the little details. I do remember that I would wear my black rubber boots over the bridge sometimes and then leave them folded in the mailbox until I was ready to come home again. You see, I had a nice pair of dancing shoes to wear, but I didn't want to muddy them up on the trip over to the hall. We may have been content without some of the finer things, but I still needed to look good.

There were no tables in the township hall, but there were benches and chairs placed around the outside of the room along the walls. Everyone brought a bag of sandwiches—egg salad or salmon sandwiches were most common—and they were combined and piled high on large serving platters to share with everyone. A large copper boiler of coffee was usually made across the concession road at the McArter house, and the men would carry it back to the hall for all to enjoy. The milk and sugar were already stirred in, so everyone got the same brew.

When the time was right, real white cups were passed around in six-quart baskets, and coffee was freely poured from big pitchers for anyone who wanted it. There was no such thing as decaf, so everyone took on full-strength regardless of the lateness of the hour. Perhaps that just meant the party would last longer, because everyone was wide awake and enjoying the dance. No one gave any thought to the fact that morning chores would come early, especially after a late night on the dance floor.

Above: Clarence and I just before a date—the height of fashion. We truly were a dapper and happy young couple.

Clarence and I had known each other for so many years before we were married that getting married just seemed like the obvious and even sensible thing to do. Once he finally popped the question (although I don't remember him getting down on one knee to ask), I started prepping for my new role as a wife and maybe even as a mother one day. Just days before we were married at St. Paul's Anglican Church in Listowel, I quit my job at the hotel in Blyth. The money I earned there was nice, but in 1949 rural Ontario, the wife stayed home and looked after the household. The regulars and a few of the seasonal workers went together and gave us a lovely wedding gift: a glass-topped coffee table and some fluffy new pillows. I was so pleased to have them. After all, we would need to set up a household of our own, and money was going to be in short supply regardless of how frugal we tried to be.

By the time I left the hotel, there was no time to dally or worry about the things we couldn't change. There was a lot to do and only a short time to do it in. We were traditional kids, from traditional families, so I moved from my hotel residence back to my parents' home for a couple of weeks before the wedding day. By this time, Daddy and my mother had sold their farm on the 5th Line of Morris Township and were living near Listowel (in Alma Township). Their new home church was St. Paul's, so that is where the ceremony was to happen. November 19 was coming fast.

We would need to be ready to settle into our new home together, and Clarence clearly needed taking care of in the meantime. I used to tease him that he was thin and that he would be lost without me. He didn't disagree, but thinking back all those years ago, he was perfect just the way he was—probably the most handsome man I had ever seen.

I recall the day we loaded up and headed off to nearby Seaforth, fifteen miles away, to buy my ring. I am not even sure where we bought our marriage licence, but Clarence must have figured it all out. There was also the matter of a dress, and not just mine. Fern White, Clarence's younger sister and my long-time friend, was to be my maid of honour, so we both needed an appropriate dress for the big day. Fern made the short trip from Brussels to Listowel so we could shop together, and after a time, we found a wonderful blue dress for me and a lovely pink one for Fern.

I had managed to put aside seventy-five dollars (more than six weeks of my wages) from my hotel earnings, so I was able to afford the dress I wanted. I plunked down fifteen dollars and thought I had the world by the tail. I had never paid so much for any article of clothing in my life, but this dress was something special.

We also planned for a wedding cake, and we grabbed a few other household essentials for the eventual "White house" that Clarence and I were setting up together. I should mention that Clarence worked with his father, John Eldon White; managed his own 50-acre farm; and took up as many jobs as he could find. He was very capable and resourceful, and he never stopped working. I knew that he would be a good provider, so I really didn't worry about things, especially since neither of us had grown up in a fancy household.

Above: My first home away from home was Clarence's fifty-acre farm on the 5th Line of Morris Township. Only two houses away from my childhood farm, this is the place where we established our first home as a couple, raised six of our seven children, and remained for the next fourteen years—until we sold and moved across the road.

Finally, the big day arrived. Clarence and I joined up with my brother, Tony, the best man, and Clarence's sister, Fern, the maid of honour, and headed off to the old Anglican Church on Wallace Street in Listowel. The ceremony was simple and traditional, and the entire affair didn't take more than a few minutes. Despite the quickness of the service, I will always remember that Clarence had to kneel at the altar. In all of our years together, that was the first and only time he was on his knees. I guess he thought I was worth it, or he would never have done it.

Daddy was at the church to give me away—something that must have been difficult for a man who was so protective of his little girl. My mother stayed at home cooking up a big goose dinner for our twenty-two expected guests. The reception was at Daddy's farm, and I remember just how many place settings there were because I set the table myself. We certainly couldn't splurge on a caterer or wedding planners, not that such things even existed in those days. We did everything ourselves.

With the help of our friends, family, neighbours, and parents, we put on a wonderful celebration that kicked off our next sixty-five years together. The meal was lovely, and all those attending had their fill. Weddings today are far more elaborate and usually involve hundreds of guests and cost thousands of dollars, but people are no happier now than we were then. That was just not the kind of thing we saw as important. I know there is a lesson there for kids today.

Above: Our wedding party on November 19, 1949. Starting on the left, my brother, Tony Ovington; my new husband, Clarence White; me (now Jane White); and Clarence's sister, Fern White. This was the first time we appeared in public as Mr. and Mrs. Clarence White.

As you might expect, our wedding celebration went on for a large part of the day. There were some wonderful gifts from our closest friends and neighbours, but nothing like you see at some weddings today. Of course, we were overwhelmed by the generosity and kindness at the time. Daddy and my mother gave us a red cow—we called her Sally—which was an amazing gift for any young farming couple to receive. Clarence's parents gave us a new Princess Pat Cook Stove and a kitchen buffet set (wow). Others gave handmade quilts, items for our new home, or even cash. People ate, laughed, and visited with each other, but at some point during the party, a few of our so-called close friends broke away and busied themselves by secretly tying several tin cans and old boots under our car.

Above: My memory of this cake is far clearer than the only picture I have of it. My wedding cake was one of the fanciest cakes I had ever seen.

It wasn't long before Clarence discovered that his precious car had been "decorated." So, after the wedding reception wrapped up and was cleaned up, we took the car, rattling cans in tow, to the Palmerston

Garage to have it properly cleaned up. Once that was done, we finally headed off on our honeymoon.

Above: Clarence's Mercury after our friends had finished with the "decorations." What a mess! Clarence had to take the car to the Palmerston Garage to have it cleaned up after the pre-shivaree antics.

As I have already said, money was in short supply (at our place and everywhere), so our honeymoon needed to be short (Clarence couldn't miss too much work) and budget appropriate. For us, that meant loading our suitcases into Clarence's Mercury and making the drive to Niagara Falls. At the time, Niagara Falls was a top honeymoon destination in the world and, as it was only 135 miles from our house, we could in theory at least make the trip in just three hours. Despite the simple-looking nature of the trip on a map, however, the journey wasn't as easy as it seemed on paper. I am not entirely sure how long it actually took us to get there, but after staying the night in a quaint little cottage along the way, the overland trip by car was still much less expensive and more realistic an option than travelling by train or plane.

It was November, and the roads to Niagara Falls were cold, covered in slush and snow, and generally unpleasant. We did a little sightseeing, but in the end, we left the city almost as quickly as we had arrived. We stayed another night at the same cottage, again enjoying the warmth of the cozy little stove in the corner. And it was a good thing the cottage was warm, because during the trip to Niagara, we discovered that someone—presumably a friend attending our wedding—had tampered with our luggage. Clarence's only pajamas had been sewn together so tightly, and with so much thread, that they were useless as bedclothes. What a shame.

With our Niagara adventure behind us, we spent one night with Daddy and my mother in their home near Listowel. The next day, after a hearty Irish breakfast, we loaded up some furniture—like my own bedroom set—and made the trip, for the first time as a newlywed couple, home to our own 50-acre farm.

❦

A short time after we were settled in our new home, a few friends and neighbours hosted a dance for us in the upstairs of the Town Hall, where the Brussels Legion is today. I am not sure if it was called a wedding shower, but it was a lot of fun. Just like the community dances of my youth, everyone brought sandwiches to share, and coffee was made in the large copper boiler next door and poured into glass cups for all to freely enjoy. We danced and enjoyed the live orchestra, and in the end, I was shocked when I learned that the event had raised $125 for us, an astounding amount of money in 1949. This wonderful gift would help us to better outfit our cozy new home.

Just when we were thinking how lucky we were to have such good friends, that notion was shattered by a strange custom known as a *shivaree*. Basically, a shivaree is when some of the wedding guests (close friends and neighbours) would return after a party ended, uninvited, and gain entry into the home of the newlywed couple. In an effort to be as disruptive as possible, once inside the home, the guests would typically bang pots and pans, mess up the house, raid the pantry, move furniture outside, and generally cause mischief and hellery.

It was no secret that I was always one for a practical joke, or even a bit of good-natured trickery, but I really don't understand why people followed the custom. I mean, filling someone's shoes with marbles, like I was known to do in my younger days, was one thing, but plunging an entire house into utter chaos is quite another. At least, that was my story when I was the one on the receiving end of a shivaree. But if I am being honest, I must confess that I may have repaid the tradition both before and after my own wedding. Notwithstanding my own concerns, it was to be expected, and unfortunately a few cans under the car (as we dealt with following the wedding reception) was just the beginning.

The dance was only a few days past when, late one night, only a short time after we hit the hay, we heard the anticipated and much-dreaded sounds of a noisy and wild group of drunken "well-wishers" stumbling their way into the yard and then through the door. We didn't lock the door in those days, so they just marched right in. They banged an old saw blade with a hammer for effect and demanded food. I scrambled to make enough salmon sandwiches and coffee for the mob while Clarence worked, to no avail, to contain the bedlam.

By the time the night was over, our kitchen floor was covered with debris, our pantry and closet contents were strewn about, and our upstairs bed had found its way out through the window into the yard. Clarence's father was absolutely furious when he found out the next day, but after hours of mopping the unfinished wood floors, and washing and drying our bedding and clothes, all that foolishness was finally behind us. I guess that made it official: the wedding celebrations were finally over, and now real life started.

Looking back, I really am thankful that we didn't have much set up when our friends hit us with the shivaree. It meant that nothing important was damaged, and there simply wasn't much in the way of furniture to move or mess up. You see, our house was simple but cozy. We had a couple of odd chairs, a small table, a good Princess Pat Cook Stove in the kitchen, a bed with a mattress upstairs, and a bed with no mattress downstairs. Who could ask for more?

As I remember, a week or so after the wedding, we made the trip to Stratford and used the money from the dance to make some much-needed purchases for our home. We bought a second-hand dining room outfit, some floor coverings, and a brand-new studio couch. Our house was still simple and cozy, but we had everything we needed, and we were truly happy. Together, we watched as the final days of 1949 slipped away into memory.

CHAPTER 7

SALLY, SOME CHICKENS, AND TWO SOWS

Children are gifts of God. It is God's way of compensating us for growing older.—An Old Irish Saying

As 1950 dawned on our little 5th Line farm, Clarence and I set to work scratching out a modest existence for the two of us. We didn't have much by way of extras, and we worked hard for everything we had, but we were happy in our youthful simplicity. We were never big farmers, nor was that really ever part of our plan. Our intention was simply to earn our living in the same way our parents had: by the sweat of our brow. Farming seemed the logical way to do it. It was what we knew.

In the months after we were married, the entirety of our stock was a few chickens, two sows, and Sally, the cow my parents had given us for a wedding present. The best we could muster was eggs, milk, and meat from the barn; some fresh vegetables from the garden; and apples from the trees. We were very good gardeners, and I canned and preserved whatever I could. If nothing else, we always had food on the table.

Every now and again, Clarence would wander home with some fresh fish wrapped in newspaper. It was supposed to be a real treat, so I would prepare and cook it up for our next meal, but secretly I never really cared for fish. But as much as I didn't care for fish, I disliked some of the prep work for other meals even more. I can clearly remember the time that I needed to kill an old hen for our meal that night. Clarence was often away, so I needed to step up and do the job myself—from flock to pot. What a terrible job. In fact, I killed two hens that day: my first and my last. Never again.

Clarence used to joke that he "always had a farm but never had anything to farm it with." There was truth to this, so he made ends meet by working with his father, doing farm work for others, driving a milk truck, delivering feed for Top Notch, and eventually, by taking a job with Hydro. This all meant that Clarence was often away, so I did my best to keep things up and running at home—and not just in the house.

Above: Clarence takes a short break from working on our first farm. There was never a shortage of work to do, and Clarence wasn't one to sit idle or quit early.

Our old barn was far from new, and it needed lots of maintenance, work, and attention, but it was central to life on our farm. Like farmers today, every time we had an extra nickel in our purse, we pumped it back into the farm for materials, feed, stock, or equipment, and that didn't even account for our labour. That was just the way of it, and it was what we knew.

But not everything was ramshackle. We had a windmill in the yard that ran the water pump to the barn. This made life so much easier for most of the year, but as it drew from a shallow-dug well, we needed to plan for the dry spells that often hit us in the hottest summer months. When the water table was low, water needed to be drawn by pail and toted to the barn from the river that cut across the back of the property. The animals were always thirsty, and they didn't seem to care that the shallow well was dry or that pailing water from the river in the extreme heat was heavy work. Perhaps this was all getting me ready for my future role as a mother of seven children.

That dug well might have been a godsend, but it was also one of the elements on our fledgling farm that we worked hard to upgrade early on. We knew that a drilled well would give us access to a much larger and more reliable water supply, so we made that a priority. I can still remember that drilling a well was going to cost about $300—a massive amount of money in those days and not easy to come by, especially for two kids without a "real job" or a credit history.

We talked to the bank in Brussels, but they wanted no part in our plans. I guess they thought lending so much money to a young couple starting out was just too risky. Clarence's stubborn pride meant that he refused to have his father co-sign for the loan; we would make our own way, thank you very much. Eventually, after a lot of fancy talking, a bank in Seaforth saw their way to help us out. Later that same year, Hopper Well Drilling appeared with its rig in the yard, and so ended the days of our shallow-dug well running dry. That was now a thing of the past.

Above: The actual document we received in 1959 from the drilling contractor. Getting a drilled well was a big deal in those days, and it was important to have all the paperwork in order before the work started.

The new well changed a lot, but there was still so much to do, and nothing was especially inexpensive or easy when we started out. Sure, there were many elements of farm life that were the same then as they are now, but a lot was different too. For example, we had a tractor, but it was nothing like what you see on the fields today. Farms were much smaller then, but so was everything else. Machines and fuel cost money, while our own muscle power was free. This meant that we did as much as we could by hand and with what we had available. We wasted nothing.

For example, when I was a child, I can remember having a swill pail in the kitchen. We dumped all the scraps and household garbage into that dreadful bucket. Things like dishwater (with very little soap), eggshells, and thinly peeled potato skins all found their way into that pail and then out to the hens as a hot mash. There wasn't a lot that made its way into the pail—as Daddy was always vigilant that the potato peelings were razor thin so as not to waste good potatoes—but what did see the pail was not thrown away.

As a child, I disliked that pail because it was stinky and sour, but as a married teen now in charge of my own budget, I learned how important stuff like that was. If there was no mash to be had, then we needed to buy hen food from our already hollow purse. It was usually easier to stir up the unappealing mash than it was to find extra cash, so my views on a swill pail quickly changed.

I didn't, however, change my mind on everything. I still hated washing the cream separator, even if it was a necessary evil. This small, gravity-fed appliance skimmed the cream off the raw milk we got from Sally and the other cows that we had been able to add to our herd. We fed cattle each year for an old farmer, and we often would take a heifer or two in trade for some of the money we would have otherwise been paid, allowing us to eventually grow our herd to eight. This allowed us to use the milk and cream separately and for different things, but it also meant that I needed to fetch, by pail, warm water to the barn each day to scrub the many small disks and parts of the machine. Winter (when the water was often frozen) or summer, the device needed to be kept sparkling, as the milk was being used on our own table, for the children. But it was a fussy and time-consuming job that I disliked.

Above: Even as time passed, work on the farm continued. Whether drawing wood and water, or feeding livestock and growing vegetables, we did what we needed to do with what we had ready at hand. This picture, while taken many years after we left the farm, captures us with our sleeves still rolled up to keep ahead of the work.

The barn may have been central to the farm, but the house was central to the daily lives of our family, and it was mostly my domain and my job to keep everything stocked and running like a top. Clarence was often away working, and on the evenings or weekends when he wasn't at work, he enjoyed his time socializing over drinks with the boys at the local pub or pool room. Because of this, I worked hard to make our house a home, but this too had its own unique set of challenges.

For example, until about 1953, there was no electricity or running water to the house. And even when we finally managed to get these little "luxuries," the hydro was just on the main floor, and the water tap in the kitchen only ran cold. Some years later, during the time when he stayed with us to convalesce from a bout of ill health and a lengthy stay in the hospital, Daddy built a stone drain to take the water away from the kitchen. Boy, we really had it made then.

I know this sounds like we lived in poverty back in the Stone Age, but this couldn't be further from the truth. This was just how it was for most people in those days. Besides, since I never had those little extras before, I didn't even miss them. How could I miss what I never had? Although I do admit to liking those extras once I learned to live with modern conveniences. For example, once we finally had hydro, I remember that the first thing I bought was a small electric bottle warmer. It was so nice being able to quickly warm a bottle for those late-night feedings without stoking the fire in the stove. I think I doubled my sleep time with that one appliance.

We did eventually get a phone—a party line—so at least staying in touch with my mother and friends was easy enough to do when Clarence was away at work with the car. It was easy to feel isolated at home alone on the farm otherwise, but I loved our wee home, warts and all. The old farmhouse was blistering hot in the summer and ice cold in the winter. No one had air conditioning in those days, unless you count opening all the windows to the outside breeze as AC. In the winter, we heated with wood, and sometimes coal, but the stove couldn't make the whole house cozy and warm without first making the room with the stove blistering hot. I always said the wind blew in one side of the house and out the other; and back then, snowing, and blustery rural Ontario winters were truly something to see and feel. Like everything else, you get used to it and you make do. After all, as a young and newly married couple, we could always snuggle if things got too cold in the winter.

<hr />

The winter of 1950 must have been especially cold, as it was March of 1951 when Sidney Eldon White, my little man, arrived on the scene. Eldon is a name that comes from the White side of the family. Both Clarence and his father, John Eldon White, carried the middle name Eldon, so we decided to keep that tradition alive. While it is true that Clarence seldom held our babies, and he never changed a diaper in his life, he was as happy as I had ever seen him when our new son arrived in the home office of Dr. Myers.

From the beginning, Sid was our pride and joy, and his arrival changed our young family forever. Being a parent in the 1950s wasn't easy. We were new to the job, and as every parent knows, even when grandparents are helpful and involved, we needed to learn along the way because children don't come with an owner's manual or an instruction book. We made lots of silly and overly protective new-parent mistakes, but Sid was a good boy who always wanted to please us, and that made our job as parents a little easier. I say *easier*, but not entirely without some storms and bumps.

Speaking of storms, when I took on the task of maintaining our home, I could not have imagined the events that would take place in May of 1953. One evening, a large tornado tore its way through a wide part of southern Ontario. We didn't have smart phone alarms, weather forecasts, or much early warning of any kind at the time, so the first sign of trouble was a loud rumbling that shook the house. Clarence knew immediately what was happening, but it took me a bit longer to clue in.

My first instinct was to snatch Sid out of his crib and head for cover in the basement. Clarence took charge without missing a beat. He yelled out for me to stay still and let the baby sleep. Clarence seemed to somehow know that we were not in any real danger, so there was no point in waking the baby in the middle of the night. The storm blew past in just a few short seconds, and we were safe again—terrified but safe. I can still hear the sound the driving rain made as it came through into the upstairs through a new hole in the roof.

We later learned that, in addition to the damage to the house roof, the storm had stripped some of the steel sheets from the barn. But all in all, we were lucky that night. We were wet and shaken (I was still so upset the next day that Sid and I went with Clarence on the milk run just to feel safe), but otherwise, all three of us were in one piece.

The same was true for the small flock of pullets Clarence had amassed by barter. We kept the birds in the barn, and the next morning we found them splashing and floating about, so we had to scoop them out of the water by hand and place them on higher ground. Notwithstanding the saying "as mad as an old wet hen," they were all fine. I guess you could say no harm, no fowl.

I also remember once when Clarence brought home two little pigs for Sid. The pigs, another acquisition by barter, were runts. This means they were the smallest in their litter and generally needed more help to survive than the others in the brood. We brought them in the house where it was warm and where we could keep a close eye on them, and they became great friends with wee Sid.

Baby pigs are cute, and they are actually quite smart. They would follow Sid around and even lay down beside him, not unlike what a dog would do. Eventually, the pigs grew larger, and they needed to live in the barn, but even that didn't stunt the friendship they had with our Sid. What did stop it was when the two pigs suddenly vanished one day. Sid was shattered, but what he didn't know was that one of his pigs died of natural causes, and the other made for a wonderful pork dinner for someone. I can't just recall how we explained the absence, but we managed to get by it anyhow.

The pig incident happened the same winter that we moved our cook stove from the kitchen into the living room in an attempt to limit the space we needed to heat. We didn't have enough wood to heat the house for the entire winter, so we used Alberta coal that year. To keep our costs down, we closed up the kitchen and moved into the smaller space with our stove in the corner. The Princess Pat Cook Stove that we had been given as a wedding gift pumped out so much heat that we nearly roasted, even on the coldest and snowiest nights. In fact, it was so hot that Sid was sick and irritable for the entire winter. We learned our lesson that year and would not make the same mistake again.

Above: There was never a shortage of snow during those old-time winters. It piled up and made travel a challenge and farm chores a pain, but it was always a real playground for our children in their younger days. Here is a picture of our youngest looking down from a snowbank circa 1970.

That first winter notwithstanding, my little man was a healthy, happy, and helpful child who enjoyed working hard and with his hands right from the start. He had a natural curiosity and his own unique personality, which emerged early on. He may even have inherited some of his father's determination. Sid always liked the outdoors and toy guns, and as the years passed, he took to fishing and hunting for fun, for recreation, and especially for solitude.

He did, however, just as I had done with a short-haired hound in my own youth, take to a little beagle he named Bruno. Sid just loved his little dog, and the two of them were best friends and constant companions for years. Eventually, we lost Sid's Bruno in a lightning strike. The strike followed along the chain and took the dog, but that was not the first brush with tragedy for old Bruno.

Several years earlier, we'd had a serious barn fire. You see, for years, Clarence had fed pigs on contract. The money was nice, but Clarence also felt our boys needed some work and responsibilities around the farm, and pigs were his answer. It worked well for a long time, and as Sid got older, he though raising pigs sounded like a good way to make some money, so he filled our old L-shaped barn with a few sows. The idea was simple enough, but as they say, life is what happens when you are making other plans.

One day, despite the fact that both Sid and I had carefully checked on the sows through the day, a heat lamp being used to keep the baby pigs warm got knocked over and took fire. We lost everything except for old Bruno, and he only just survived. When he spotted the fire, he panicked and headed for shelter in the henhouse attached to the barn. Some men in the yard saw him and pulled the terrified dog from the fire using the chain around his collar. Bruno seemed to smoke and smoulder in the snow once he was free of the flames, and he had a raspy wheeze for the rest of his days. Farming sure isn't for the faint of heart.

Sid's desire for solitude and his hands-on nature are probably why he didn't care much for school. He was always smart enough, but he never gravitated to books or classes, and he was always eager to start into the world of work. Sid only completed as much school as he absolutely had to before plunging headlong down his own life path. He never looked back.

Above: Greyhounds are lovely pets. This is my own childhood pal, Ring. Dogs and other animals were

always a big part of my life on the farm, and for some of my own children (like Sid), pets were true and loyal friends.

Years later, as an adult, Sid became an exceptional carpenter who was known for his attention to detail and craftsmanship—an interest that probably took root at some point in his father's workshop. Sid loved to tinker and to be with his dad. Clarence was a great woodworker who, I like to think, inspired Sid onto his chosen path, but Sid took that trade to the next level by making it his profession. Sid's work is beautiful, and the quality of that work stands for itself.

This reputation and Sid's strong work ethic have allowed him to make a good living; to establish a home with his wife, Melody; and to make his own way in the world. Clarence and I have always been proud of Sid. It has been a real joy to watch him become the person he is today.

Chapter 8

Glad as the Shamrocks

May there always be work for your hands to do,
May your purse always hold a coin or two,
May the sun always shine on your windowpane,
May the rainbow be certain to follow the rain,
May the hand of a friend always be near you,
May God fill your heart with gladness to cheer you.
—An Old Irish Saying

Sid was our first child, but he was not to be the last bundle of joy in our fledgling home. In the years following Sid's arrival, Clarence and I welcomed six additional members of the White family and worked to give each a safe and happy place to grow up. It was seldom easy, but forgetting the normal hiccups and challenges that all families encounter and deal with when raising children, I wouldn't change anything or send any of them back.

We have been fortunate to see each of our children grow to adulthood, find a life partner, and have children and even grandchildren of their own. Without exception, we are proud of the people they have become and the paths they have chosen.

It was September of 1953 when we again made the trip to Dr. Myers' house for another special delivery. Our little family was about to expand again, and this time, we were to be blessed with a beautiful and dark-haired little girl we called Judy Lavare. The name came about as Clarence liked the name *Lavare* and I thought *Judy* was a pretty name that would be fitting for the newest White. Judy was such a cute wee thing with her rosy cheeks—especially on those cold winter mornings—and a little kiss curl dipping down on her forehead. I am not sure any pictures exist from those early days with Judy, but I remember that curl well, and it still makes me smile whenever the image pops into my head.

I also remember that I didn't make the same mistake I'd made with Sid by keeping Judy and the house too warm through the first winter. After Sid's winter of sniffles and coughs, I came to believe that a cool house creates healthy kids. The winter of 1953 was terribly cold, so it allowed me to put my theory to the test. Thinking back, my bones can still feel the wind whistling through the thin plaster walls and poorly insulated attic of our old farmhouse. It's a wonder we didn't all freeze in our beds, but somehow, we survived.

Rather than rev up the Princess Pat Cook Stove, I had Sid snuggle in with Clarence and me, and I bundled Judy up in a little pink snowsuit and lots of blankets for the nights. She slept peacefully in a basket by our bed and never seemed to be bothered that we could usually see our breath in the crisp air each morning as we opened our eyes. I am sure today's parenting books would frown on that kind of thing, but it worked for us. Judy was not sick even once that winter, so I guess I will leave today's parenting wisdom to today's parents.

The year 1953 was also when we finally got hydro in the house. This was a big step forward, not unlike when we drilled the deeper well. I remember because the very first electric appliance I ever purchased was a small bottle warmer that made Judy's night feedings so much easier than when Sid was a baby. I used to have to stoke and heat the stove every time I needed a bottle, but by 1953, we had entered the modern era at the White house, and it was grand. I also recall that we ran an extension cord up the stairs and over the wood banister, which gave us upstairs lighting for the first time ever. I am not sure if that arrangement would pass any kind of electrical home inspection today, but Clarence and I thought we were in heaven with all this new-found luxury and modern convenience.

From the very beginning, Judy was a natural charmer. As the years passed, she became my little shadow. She was always happy and so eager to help around the house. In fact, she was a little maid and a helpful mother hen to the other children. She was good in school, and her instinctive childhood desire to care for others followed her into adulthood. It made her a natural fit for her eventual profession as a nurse.

Years later, Judy married Ross Somers, and they had two children (Scott and Heather). If you ask them, I am sure they too would admit that Judy's mother hen tendencies never really went away. As a mother, I always thought that it was a great trait for her to have. I know that I was lucky to have her helping out as our young family continued to expand.

⌘

And expand it did, this time in December of 1954. I remember that the day was clear but windy and cold as we made our way to see Dr. Myers at his nearby home. Shortly after we got there, Richard Kenneth, named after two of his uncles, arrived on the scene kicking and screaming in true White fashion. Always untiring and determined, our boy, who was quite slight in his youth, was tough as nails from the start—so much so that he defied the odds, the neighbours' whispers of impending trouble, and even my own deepest and worst unspoken fears when he successfully battled whooping cough that first year.

Whooping cough was a real threat in those days. There is a vaccination for it today, but no such option existed back then. It is such a terrible thing in little ones, and it took so many. They cough endlessly and even violently, and there is little a parent can do to help or to ease their struggle. There were days when Rick could barely take a breath without bursting into a coughing fit. I spent so many sleepless nights up and down with him in the rocking chair and walking the floors, just trying to help him take his next breath. It still shakes me when I think back to what he went through.

Fortunately, he managed to recover, and once he did, he never looked back. From that moment on, Rick was always a bit of a whirlwind. I remember one time when we loaded up the car and headed to a beach on the Lake Huron shoreline. After a day running about on the sand with Rick and our other children, and another couple and their little girl, Clarence was drained from worry and fit to be tied. He vowed to "never again" go back to the water with the children alone. He stubbornly kept that promise, but years later we did go back to the lake the odd time with friends. As I remember it, though, Clarence only joined us after he was done with work for the day.

You see, on that first trip with wee Rick, we had dressed him in a pair of little red swim trunks in the hope that he would be easier to see in a crowd of beachgoers. Unfortunately, everyone else seemed to have had the same great idea. Clarence, ever the worrier, was nearly frazzled from trying to keep watch over Rick as the toddler buzzed around everywhere—on the beach, in and out of the water every few seconds, on the swings, and up and down the slide with dozens of other children. Rick was fast on his feet, which generally helped him torment his brother and sister on a regular day, but it also made him difficult to contain on the busy beach. His father was forever scarred by the experience.

We had lots of experiences where Rick helped turn our hair grey. I am reminded of one occasion in particular when Rick was snooping around (as he often did) and found a partial box of Warfarin. As any farmer knows, even today, this is a popular brand of rat poison that most have hidden away on a shelf somewhere. In this case, young Rick managed to find some when he was unsupervised, and by the time his discovery came to my attention, the poison was spilled, and there was no way to know for sure if Rick had eaten any.

I was frightened beyond words, but as they say, there was no time to do nothing. I couldn't risk that Rick hadn't eaten any, so I grabbed him up and forced him to drink warm saltwater brine until he threw up again and again. By the time I was done with him, there was no doubt that he was Warfarin-free—but as I recall, I was not his favourite person for at least a few days following the mess.

He eventually got over it, and that was a good thing, because he was always into something. Every time you turned your back on him, he managed to find mischief. From tormenting his siblings whenever the chance arose to the time his bedroom window painfully dropped down on both his hands—something I heard happen all the way from the garden—Rick had a spark that led him to little bouts of mischief and, on occasion, minor trouble.

It should also be said that Rick could switch out his mischief maker's hat in favour of a pair of kid gloves. He was forever trailing back to the farm with found critters that needed a home and some TLC. Whether a nest of baby rabbits or our under-the-table dog Blackie, Rick was often the head lobbyist for all things cute and fluffy. He might not always show it, but he has a big heart that makes his mother proud.

Notwithstanding the hellery of his younger days, like his brothers and sisters, Rick grew up to be hard-working, honest, and dependable. He is someone I can always count on to this very day. He now works for his local municipality, contributing daily to the betterment of his community and travelling around on many of the same streets I would have trod upon in my own youth. He is a family man who is well-liked and enjoys nothing more than a good laugh and some quality time with his partner, Debbie Keffer; their children, Julie and Cheryl; and their grandchildren.

Above: A moment of calm with my three eldest children. Sid, Judy, and Rick are dressed up and ready for a trip to town.

Despite the busy and growing nature of our young family, Rick was not to be the final addition to our clan. Less than three years later, in April of 1957, we welcomed a fourth bundle of joy to the White house—another boy. Samuel Keith John was the first of our children to be born in a hospital rather than at Dr. Myers' home office. The newest White was named after his two grandfathers: Samuel for Daddy and John for Clarence's father. Despite his lengthy formal moniker, we decided to just call him Keith.

I am not sure why we decided on Keith; I guess he looked like a Keith to us. I do remember that it was unusually hot that spring day. I also remember that my mother and I worked tirelessly all morning to clean up the yard. Once the work was done and the yard looked its best, we headed off to Wingham Hospital for the big delivery.

I can still picture baby Keith in my mind's eye. He was roly-poly in that way that makes a new baby especially cute and cuddly. It was perhaps good that he had some extra padding, because as he learned to walk and eventually to run, we discovered that he was far less graceful than we might have hoped. In fact, he was downright clumsy and spent more time on the floor than on his feet. I used to joke that he would trip over a piece of straw if you let him—and there were lots of times when he went down.

Despite the many bumps, bruises, and cuts he often sported on his knees, elbows, and chin, he was always a happy kid who refused to let a slip or fall keep him down. In many ways, I think his tumbles may have toughened him up, because he soon learned how to take a fall without shedding a tear. He also learned rather quickly that his sly little smile could get him out of lots of trouble if he used it at just the right time—and use it he did.

If I am being honest, aside from his lack of grace, Keith was a relatively easy child to raise. When he was a baby, I would give him his cow's milk in a Coke bottle with a rubber nipple stretched over the top. That always seemed to do the trick. Even as he grew older, he was generally a happy kid, but happy doesn't mean he was entirely trouble-free. There was the time when he and Clarence both got the mumps at the same time. What a disaster! They were so sick, and they both readily soaked up all the TLC and attention at home. I am not sure who was the bigger baby, but the two of them eventually recovered none the worse for wear.

Keith was a content child who was happy just to be part of whatever was going on—like the time Clarence and I threw the four kids in the car and decided on a family outing to the Huron Pioneer Threshers and Steam Show in Blyth. Keith was just a babe in arms at the time, but an outing to the annual show was always a favourite destination for the White family. In fact, attending this huge agricultural fair and showcase of antique and steam-driven farm equipment was the kind of thing that many families did and still do each September on the first weekend after Labour Day. A typical visit would involve watching a parade, viewing the crafts and produce, taking in some live old-time music, and enjoying snacks of fresh popcorn, hand-rolled ice cream, or maybe even some cotton candy.

This all sounds great, but in September of 1957, our pilgrimage was somewhat different than what other families may have experienced that day. You see, the rusty floorboards in our old car were thin as a screen, and after the twenty-minute trek down the gravel and dirt backroads (we took the gravel roads to evade traffic and unwanted attention from the police because of the poor condition of the car), we were all covered with a thick layer of dust when we arrived. Spitting and frantically patting our clothes and hair clean, we must have looked like a family of snowmen as we emerged from our old wreck of a car in the parking lot at the Blyth fairgrounds. We weren't always pretty, but we were together, and we never failed to make the best out of what we had.

As Keith grew up, that boyish smile kept him out of several scrapes, but there were a few missteps worthy of note. For example, I remember the day when I slipped out to the woodpile for a few seconds only to return to a disaster. There stood Keith, cute smile stuck squarely on his face, hoping that I would not notice that he had dumped an entire can of baby powder over onto his baby sister's head. Another mess for me to clean up.

Speaking of which, there was also the time when Keith tried his hand at making hard apple cider. He was in his teens, so you would think he would have some more sense. He gathered and crushed the apples and then collected the murky brown juice in a few old bottles he found around the house. He placed the closed-up bottles carefully in his dresser, presumably to age and to allow the sugars to ferment into alcohol.

As you may know, fermenting apple cider will off-gas and expand when not burped properly. Too much expansion creates pressure and causes glass bottles to explode without warning. On this occasion, I think one could say that Keith's failing skills as a brew master tripped him up in a big way. As expected, the concoction did indeed expand and explode. The brew filled his dresser, soaking his clothes with the stinky and sticky brown cider, and it covered the floor with a terrible and foul-smelling liquid. Cute smile or not, thus ended his illustrious career as a cider-ist. Fortunately, the experience didn't have any lasting impact on his future, although his ears were probably ringing for a bit.

Today, Keith works hard, but he also plays hard. Now that his cider-making days are behind him, he fills his time with his partner, Jayne Ross; their children, Kevin, Shannon, Kelly, Amy, and Candice; and their grandchildren. They enjoy watching their wonderful grandkids play hockey and baseball. Keith is a good man, and it is possible that his only serious fault is his absolute devotion to the Ford Motor Company. But nobody's perfect, right, Keith?

Above: The first four White children: Sid, Judy, Rick, and Keith.

With three boys and only one girl in the house, I found myself secretly and quietly hoping for the gender balance to shift. My wee Judy was now nearly five years old, so another baby girl in the house might not be a bad idea. Well, it wasn't long until I had the opportunity to put that thinking to the test.

Another trip to Wingham Hospital in July of 1958, and we returned home with our little blonde-haired baby girl, Mary Colleen— or Colleen, as we called her. She was named for her two grandmothers (both named Mary), so, as expected, they were both thrilled when she arrived. They loved her dearly and doted over her, which was good, because she was colicky and required loads of patience, care, and attention at first.

I could never let her just sit there and cry, so I held her, carried her on my hip, and rocked her almost constantly for those first weeks. I know there were some who felt that I spoiled her, that I should just let her cry it out in her bed. That Old World parenting wisdom might have been the thinking of my mother's era, but it was not how I was going to handle things as a determined mother with more than seven years of parenting experience under my apron.

Eventually, Colleen grew out of the colic and was a good and happy girl. She was content and liked to play with her dolls, with her friends, and with her brothers and sisters, but she certainly had a mind of her own from the very beginning. I always liked that about her. You never had to guess if you had aggravated her, but she was generally slow to make up after a blow-out. She certainly had her favourite things to do and her favourite people in any crowd.

I guess you could say that she inherited her father's strong will and was never afraid to stand her ground against the others when she felt the situation called for it—something that she deemed necessary on more than one occasion. But don't take my word for it; just ask her brothers what happened when they crossed her (or any of my girls, for that matter).

Even as a young girl, Colleen had so many abilities. She was a great cook, loved to clean house, was generally very tidy, enjoyed order in all things, and typically knew just how she wanted things done. It was not uncommon for her to sternly remind her brothers whenever they crossed a line or failed to see things her way. We used to quip, "Why would you do something the wrong way when you could just do it the 'White way'?" Despite knowing better and knowing the consequences when they stepped out of line, Sid, Rick, and Keith liked to push Colleen's buttons sometimes, and this often brought them into conflict.

Colleen didn't let the uneven gender numbers in the household deter her, nor did it matter that she was the youngest. She knew what she wanted and wasn't afraid to push back. This was and is still her superpower.

In addition to her father's fire, Colleen inherited my storytelling abilities. She had a real charm about her, and she was genuinely sweet— even if that sweetness was tested to the limit a time or two. For example, I remember the day Colleen took to flying. I was rushing to finish up the chores in the barn because we were planning a trip away to town, and everyone was getting dressed in their best for an outing. I expect

Judy was probably coordinating the effort in the house while I was still finishing up in the barn. We both lost sight of young Colleen, and at some point, she came looking for me.

I don't know if it was just bad timing or a simple coincidence, but our old pet cow Sally was leaving the barn just as Colleen was trying to enter through the same doorway. Colleen must have surprised the normally friendly animal when they met up on the sill. The surprise caused Sally to lurch forward and jerk up her head, catching Colleen's clothing in her horns. In one swift and powerful action, Sally set off a huge commotion as she fired wee Colleen—dressed in her Sunday best—screaming through the air toward her eventual soft-landing splat in the nearby manure pile.

As to be expected, the furious Colleen was a terrible and smelly heap—yet another item on Judy's perpetual clean-up task list. Colleen, who loved order and cleanliness, was none too happy about the situation. No one was hurt that day, but Colleen was quite out of sorts following the ordeal—although we all laugh about her sudden flight all these years later.

While Colleen has my daddy's and Clarence's fire, she was and is also someone who cares deeply for her friends and family. I can't help but remember the time after she first met a young pig farmer named Murray McNichol. It didn't take us long to figure out that Murray was Colleen's dream boy, because he was all she talked about for quite some time. I also noticed that the word *Murray* was suddenly being scribbled on nearly everything around the house (reminds me of my own younger days and my own dream boy). I wonder if she still has the little pillow with his name sewn on it? I wonder if Murray ever knew she had such a thing? I wonder if I just let the cat out of the bag?

She may or may not have the pillow, but she certainly kept hold of Murray, and they have now been married for more than 45 years. They have three grown children (James, Julie, and Michelle) and several wonderful grandchildren. They still farm together and own a lovely cottage on Lake Huron that I often visit. Colleen is a devoted, happy, and hard-working woman. She would do anything for you. I am certainly lucky to have her help when I need it and her friendship always.

Chapter 9

A Turning of the Page

May God grant you always a sunbeam to warm you,
A moonbeam to charm you
A sheltering angel so nothing can harm you.
—An Old Irish Saying

As the 1960s dawned on our 50-acre farm on the 5th Line of Morris Township, all seemed to be as it should be. Clarence and I were celebrating more than ten wonderful years of marriage. We had good friends to share happy times with. We had five healthy young children, and both of us had the benefit of our parents being active and important parts of our lives. We were not rich, nor did we live a lavish lifestyle, but we had all that we needed and much of what we wanted. Life was grand, but as we marched headlong into 1961, we could never have imagined just how much things would change and how quickly those changes would come upon us.

It all started on a normal Monday morning in September of 1961. The day was still and cool—only about 50 degrees Fahrenheit—which meant it was nearly perfect for heavy outside work. Lucky for us, because the day promised to be a busy one, as the silage-fillers were scheduled to be on the property to do their work that afternoon. This meant the house was already a busy hub of activity well before the first rays of the morning sun popped over the horizon.

The kitchen was abuzz with activity, and the wonderful smells of cooking food filled the air well ahead of breakfast. There were snacks, drinks, and hearty meals to prepare in advance of the workers' arrival, so there was no time to languish under the covers no matter how heavy our eyes. In those days, you needed to feed and water the help on days like this, and everything needed to happen smoothly and on time, so they weren't delayed getting back to their work. Mechanical breakdown and the threat of bad weather were already potential barriers to the work being done, so the last thing you needed was something avoidable like a late lunch preventing the men from doing what they needed to do in the limited time they had to do it. As busy as things were in the kitchen, Clarence was even busier getting things prepped and ready in the barn.

Daddy brought my mother over in the car to help with the meal preparations and child-minding. We were also joined by my dear friend and neighbour Bell Workman. In those days, it was common for neighbours and extended family members to adopt an all-hands-on-deck approach to a large task or work bee, and this was one of those times.

Bell was more than just a good friend and neighbour. She was an absolute godsend to have on hand, especially on this particular day. As it turned out, she and my mother would be doing far more than just helping, as I needed to make yet another trip to the hospital. Promising to remain at the house for a couple of days, my support duo stoically stepped up to manage both the children and the extra domestic duties connected to the work bee as I headed to the Wingham Hospital for the arrival of baby number six.

Above: Clarence readies the tractor while Daddy, pipe in hand, looks on.

I can still remember that Daddy was excited for another grandchild to arrive. Daddy and my mother loved their grandchildren dearly. Likewise, our children were always close with both Daddy and my mother, and they all enjoyed spending time together, so I expected that all would go smoothly while I was away.

In addition to his joyful anticipation, Daddy was also determined to do something extra-special for me, the new mom-to-be. After a quick inspection of the happenings on the farm, Daddy headed out on the hunt for a fresh leg of lamb. I am not entirely sure why he had his heart set on buying me lamb—I am not even a big fan of lamb—but his motives were pure, and I appreciated the thought. As an aside, his hunt was not entirely successful, but he did return to the house later that day with a rather large ham for my mother to prepare.

With everything at home well in hand, I loaded into the car with my long-time friend turned sister-in-law Fern and her then-husband Ray, and we set off toward the hospital. Of course, in those days, the only man allowed in the delivery room was the doctor, so it wouldn't have been usual or helpful to have Clarence come with us—not that he would have been able to leave the farm unattended anyway.

Fortunately, it wasn't long after we arrived at the hospital that the gender balance in the White house was finally even for the first time since Clarence and I were married. Susan Jane was the prettiest little thing you ever saw. In fact, she was so beautiful that I named her after myself. I thought I should finally get some credit for all these babies. After all, it seemed only fitting to name someone so cute after me.

Susan was a good little girl, and as I remember, we always had lots of babysitters and people fussing and fawning over her. This made her the life of the party and the centre of attention, but it also meant that she grew to enjoy all the toadying. Eventually, she came to know that she was the apple of so many eyes, and knowing this, she sometimes liked to push her luck. She would scare the daylights out of me by holding her breath for a long time; sometimes to the point where she would even pass out (like the time she fell out of the high chair and terrified all of us). She would do this when she wanted her own way as a means of getting me to give in.

I don't know if she ever pulled that trick on her father. Maybe she knew that Clarence was more stubborn than me and probably wouldn't take too kindly to the sass. She might have been fiery, but she was also smart. We eventually broke her of holding her breath as a threat tactic, but she held on to her determined nature even until today.

This is a good thing because, as the youngest to this point, she had three older brothers to deal with. I seem to recall that she never took a backseat to her rough-and-tumble brothers, and like my other girls, she wasn't afraid to stand her ground with them. She may have been cute, but she was no pushover.

But things didn't always go her way, although many of Susan's troubles were accidental as opposed to intentional mischief. I remember the time when she took the end of her finger off in the screen door. Her screams and the blood that poured everywhere quickly alerted us to the problem. We scooped her up and headed off to the hospital, only to be forced to return home a short time later to recover the little fingertip so it could be surgically reattached. We did have some experience with this kind of thing, though: Judy had also nipped off the end of a finger once.

With six children running about, we certainly had lots of days when wild things like that happened in the White house—and Susan was often up to her elbows in the middle of it all. I wouldn't have had it any other way.

Above: Me and my girls, left to right—Susan, Colleen, me, and Judy

Today, Susan and her husband, Carl Bondi, are happy residents of New Hamburg, Ontario. Susan retired from the nursing profession a few years back, and now they spend their days in the gym, travelling (when there are no pandemic-based travel restrictions), and visiting with their wonderful daughter, Jenni, and her husband, Raffles Cowan, in the United States. There are no grandchildren yet, but as Jenni and Raff were only married in 2019 and educational pursuits still dominate their life plans, I am sure Susan is hoping for the day when she will have the great pleasure of being a grandmother. In fact, I now hear rumblings that Susan will be promoted to Granny sooner rather than later (this year even).

In the meantime, Susan has a wonderful and fiery personality, a strong sense of humour, and a deep sense of family. These are all traits that served her in her youth and have made her a good friend and a tremendous mother. I truly love our visits and look forward to spending many more years with her, and with my other girls (and the boys too).

The story of Susan's day of birth is one of bittersweet memories. It is sweet because I had a wonderful little girl come into my life, but it is bitter because later that day, all hell broke loose around home. My mother and Bell were in the kitchen at our place and with the children,

Clarence was working with the threshers, and when Daddy left for his home in Wroxeter, all seemed to be well in hand. As a group, we had successfully managed our incredibly hectic day and probably all assumed that we were surely ready for whatever would come next.

That was, until the next morning, when a neighbour found Daddy slumped down in the driver's seat of his car. It seems that, after delivering his gift of ham to our farm—his last gift to me—Daddy returned home for the night. He successfully pulled in the drive and entered the house, but then he left again at some point. No one knows for sure why he left the house again, but he got into the car and passed away quietly in the night. Daddy was a long-time asthmatic and seasonal allergy sufferer, and he battled numerous ailments brought on by a combination of age, lifestyle choices, and personal habits. But none of us expected the end to come when it did.

Daddy's trusted and long-time doctor said it was probably general ill health and a total systems failure. The coroner said it was likely asphyxiation. Either way, my dear daddy was gone forever. Somehow everything changed in an instant.

When word finally made it to my mother, she was understandably devastated. Her partner of 35 years was gone forever. She headed for home to sort things out, but work on the farm was still underway. Clarence simply could not drop everything to deal with the crisis.

Fortunately, our wonderful friends and neighbours came forward to help, all under the watchful and capable supervision of Bell. With the exception of Sid, who was 10 at the time and able to manage with Clarence, all of the children were whisked away without a care. Neighbours even came and prepared meals so the silage-fillers would be able to eat on time and finish their work. This is one of the great things about living in a small rural community. We didn't even need to ask, but I don't know how we would have managed to get through it all without their help.

As I was still laid up in the hospital with Susan, coming home early wasn't really an option—not that I would have been of any use at home anyway. Once the silage-fillers were done with their work, Clarence made the trip to Wingham to break the awful news that Daddy was gone. Unfortunately, I'd already heard. I can still remember being terribly upset and even afraid when the nurse pulled back the curtain and unceremoniously blurted out the news that Daddy had died. When her grim face had first appeared at the door, I feared that something terrible had happened to baby Susan in the night.

Eventually, the terrible news sunk in. As was to be expected, I was not in a good state. Clarence fared no better. To put it mildly, he was not in a good twist. As the story goes, knowing it would be required for Daddy's funeral, at some point Clarence sent his suit to be cleaned. Normally, this is something that I would have taken care of, but as I was otherwise occupied, Clarence was left to fend for himself. When it came back from the cleaners, he said it smelled terribly of coal oil, but I guess he wore it anyway.

Also, he somehow had managed to take the three oldest children to get new shoes for the funeral, but when he got the children and the shoes home, there were more left shoes in the boxes than there were right shoes. I'm not sure how that all worked itself out, but I have it on good authority that each of the children had shoes for the funeral.

To top it all off, our cattle picked that very day to break through the fence, and they were off across the river grazing on turnip tops. Put another way, everything went wrong, and Clarence was fit to be tied. I expect there may have been some colourful language in the air that day.

Looking back, I was glad to have Susan but deeply upset over the other events of that day. I regret that Daddy did not get to meet Susan and her eventual younger brother, but I like to think that they felt his influence in our household just the same. All that aside, the chaos of the days following Susan's birth reminded me that, as our family was growing, my role at home was more important than it had ever been. Clarence and the children needed me, and that was fine by me. Clearly, we would need to stick together if we were going to be successful in beating back life's challenges ahead.

CHAPTER 10

THE MISSING PIECES

There's no use boiling your cabbage twice.—An Old Irish Saying

By 1963, things had normalized, and we were again dealing with the regular rhythms of daily life with six children, Clarence's jobs, and a busy farm. Despite managing things, with work and finances being what they were, we made the decision to sell our farm on the 5th Line of Morris Township. We didn't go far, but uprooting after fourteen years in one place, whether moving across the road or across the province, is still a big job. Fortunately for us, we were just moving across the road, so there was no need to pay big bucks for a moving truck.

We made the move in mid–1963 and set up in the house formerly owned by Miller McArter. The property, owned by Bill Adams at the time, was five acres, and it had a good barn and a decent house. The smaller acreage allowed us to reduce our collective debt load, which was nice, and we still had space in the house for our growing brood. Of course, I was quite familiar with the house from when I was a child. I remember that I always liked the place. It was just a couple of doors down from where I grew up, so I had often walked past the lane when I was a little girl.

Miller's mother (they called her Jean, but her proper name was Jane, like mine) used to save the funny papers for me each week. I enjoyed both the read and our conversations. She was wonderfully kind—as was her husband, Jack—but they were both gone by the time we bought the house. Her son Miller was also quite nice, and he had been so good to our family over the years. He was also a big fan of our children. He had a grandfatherly way about him.

As but one example, years after the fact, I learned that our older kids had once started the tractor on the gangway leading to the barn. I expect that they were out for a bit of a joyride, and when they were unable to enact their secret plan fully, Miller came to their rescue. As I understand it now, he took them all out for a ride and even returned the tractor to the same location afterward so as not to alert Clarence that his tractor had been on the move. Amazingly, all of them kept that secret for years.

I should perhaps clarify my earlier comment that the old McArter homestead was *decent*. It was indeed modern for the day, but by today's standards, it was still lacking. There was no running water in the house, but we soon piped it in. After all, we had become used to all the modern conveniences, like running water and hydro, so I wasn't keen to take a step back. As luck would have it, there was a windmill and a good drilled well in the yard, so we had everything we needed to make this new house a home. We could still have some animals in the barn, but with less property to tend, there would be less work at home, which would allow Clarence to focus on his off-farm jobs while I stuck close to home and kept a careful eye on the children.

Above: Our new home on five acres, but still on the 5th Line of Morris Township (now Huron County Road

16 or Morris Road). It took some work, but we would spend almost fifty years building a life here.

I wasn't what you might today call a helicopter mom, but I did worry sometimes. From the start, the kids all had a good head on their shoulders, but it's still a mother's job to worry. As the children grew up, the concern didn't fade, especially when they started to drive. When they were out on the road, I was like an old mother hen pacing and frantically waiting for her chicks to return to the nest. I guess that's all part of the parenting experience, but for the most part, driving was still some time away.

For the first few years after the big move, we burned coal in the kitchen stove to heat the place. It was delivered by a truck that would dump the dusty load into the coal window that emptied into the basement. Sadly, coal dust was just part of things on the farm. We made do for a while, but it wasn't long before we put in a new furnace and a nice in-house bathroom with hot and cold running water. That was living.

It was great to have the updated amenities, but I had been quite content with the existing backhouse out in the yard. It was so much better than what we had left at our previous home. Our facilities, prior to the in-house addition, featured an old made-up toilet. It consisted of a wooden box with a round hole in the top and a pail shoved underneath. That's what we used year-round, supplemented by the use of chamber pots overnight during the winter—something my grandchildren find odd today. The entire contraption was in the corner of the woodshed behind a wooden door. All very modern (at the time), nice, and private. I am not sure I would like to return to those days now, but at the time, it was more than enough to make me happy.

Truth be known, I was always happy with our little home. In time, we made it our own by building a two-car garage that Clarence nearly lived in. He transformed at least one bay into a nice woodworking shop where he enjoyed his hobby. He would spend hours out there making lovely shelving, cabinets, wainscoting, and other fixtures and additions to our home. Years later, he even made cedar chests for each of our children, and four beautiful china cabinets for me.

Above: Clarence in his woodworking shop with one of his many projects. This cedar chest, one of several he made, is now in the home of one of our children or grandchildren.

We had life well in hand and were settled into our routine when, in February of 1966, the White house expanded yet again. Brian George White—so named by my mother and cousin Gertie, after my uncle George—arrived safe and sound at the Wingham Hospital. Being the youngest and final member of the family, Brian was immediately everyone's pride and joy. His oldest brother Sid took a special liking to him from Day One and helped the rest of us to spoil this new baby boy. It was nice because, as we were not as busy at home, I actually had extra time to spend with Brian. This hadn't been the case with all of the children, but this time was different. In many ways, Brian was a first baby all over again.

Brian was usually a good lad, but he was full of surprises. Like the time we caught him hammering nails into a giant orange show pumpkin that Colleen had grown, washed, and carefully prepared for the Belgrave fair. The fair was a big deal in our household. I went when I was in school, and I wanted my children to have the same kind of memorable experiences. Attending was an all-day affair, and it usually started with us loading up the car with pumpkins and other special items for the competitions and shows.

As you might imagine, with so much on the line, Colleen was furious with her baby brother when he ruined her prized pumpkin. She was equally unimpressed when we discovered little bite marks in most of the raw cobs of corn that she had carefully picked and sorted for the show. Oh yes, the youngest White was always a going concern, even as he grew older.

In those days, all the boys carried pocket knives, and Brian was, as he got older, no exception. I remember that he used to sharpen his blade for hours at a time, so it was like a little razor. One day, he sliced down the backs of his father's good leather dress shoes. He caught it for that but didn't seem fazed by the angry fallout. He also didn't seem to care that Clarence's dress shoes never fit just right after that. I guess that kind of indifference to trouble is all part of being the baby of any family.

As much as Brian was the apple of everyone's eye, he certainly caused his fair share of terror for his brothers and sisters. Fortunately, as the years passed, Brian's mischief-making days grew fewer and fewer, although they are still not entirely gone. Today, just as when he was a boy, he continues to hang out in the trees (he makes his living cutting trees), to hunt, and to enjoy the company of his life partner, Cathy Goetz. Brian has two sons, Curtis and Kane, and a granddaughter— the newest edition to the White family. His sons both share his love and passion for the outdoors, for having fun, and for family.

Above: The final three White children—Colleen, Susan, and Brian – and Big Susan.

With Brian's arrival, that generation of the White family was complete, but I would be remiss if I failed to mention another special part of our family for many years. We have come to call her Big Susan, but her real name is Susan Dodds—now Susan Heron, as she is married to Paul Heron. Susan is my cousin Gertie's daughter, and over the years, she has spent many summers and holidays with us at the White house—so much so that she really became like another daughter to us. Certainly, she was and remains close with our children, who view her more like a sister than a cousin.

Susan was just another of our brood whenever she was with us. She would partake of the work and the play just like the others. She had her own unique personality, just like our seven, and she had dislikes and preferences too. For example, Susan hated picking cucumbers—not that any of the group were especially fond of the job. I am not sure why, because she was certainly not a lazy girl, but for whatever reason, she just hated that job. Maybe she just let us know more than the others?

The other kids would often pick cucumbers for pocket money and then take their profits and go shopping. We did not pay our kids a regular allowance, but when they worked, we were prepared to reward their efforts with a coin or two for their next trip to town. We also made sure they had something in their pocket when they went visiting with friends. This usually motivated the children, including Susan. She would do the required work, but it was clearly not a favourite pastime.

Today, Susan and Paul live in Port Dover, Ontario, where they have two grown children. She now wears the title of grandma too. She remains close with our family and is the source of so many wonderful memories of the time she spent with us and our children while they were growing up together.

Above: One of the family—Judy, me, Clarence, Big Susan (with her children, Katryn and Dawson), and Colleen never stopped building fun memories. In this picture, we all model hats from the giant bag of hats that Clarence brought home as a found treasure from a nearby farm auction.

Chapter 11

Buying on Instalment

It's not our job to toughen our children up to face a cruel world. It is our job to raise children who will make the world less cruel.—L. R. Knost

Even by the time our youngest was born in 1966, money was tight, and we wasted very little. Downsizing our long-time farm certainly lightened our debt load, but I wouldn't want to give the impression that we were on easy street. I suppose our thriftiness was part habit and part necessity. We still made do with less whenever we could.

We fixed or repaired what we had. Hand-me-downs were more the norm than the exception, and items such as quilts and homemade knitted mittens were the standard (something I continued to make for my grandchildren and great-grandchildren). I sometimes think of all the mending I used to do when my grandchildren visit while wearing their "distressed" jeans. Oh, how I wish 1960s fashion would have allowed our children to wear ripped jeans to school like they do today. Just think of the time and thread I would have saved not having to sew up all those torn knees and fallen hems.

Despite all of this frugality, we still had those little extras and fun family rituals that hopefully helped the children build special memories and happy times to think back on later in life. Clarence still worked a lot, and he enjoyed spending his free time in the Brussels pool room, so when the kids were little, I stuck close to home and to them. In many ways, they were my hobbies as much as they were my charges, but looking back, I wouldn't have it any other way. I can't imagine how so many moms today get on when they need to return to work so soon after the birth of a new baby. I know it is the way of things now, but I truly enjoyed being there with my children during their earliest days, months, and years.

Through the week, once the children were old enough, they went off to school. Like me in my younger days, some didn't relish the idea of school, but they all went, and they all worked hard while they were there. While they were away, I worked at things around the house, in the garden, and around our little hobby farm. The work never really stopped. I filled my days washing and mending clothes (skills I had learned at my mother's heel), keeping the house, and ensuring that everything happened as it needed to happen. In the evenings, the children did their chores before I helped them with any homework, listened to their wild stories, made their meals, and tucked them in at night. With a family of nine to feed three meals each day, there was never a shortage of cooking or preserving that needed to be done.

We usually had simple meals and snacks, but no one ever went hungry. For example, toast was always a favourite because it filled tummies without breaking the bank. Clarence, on the other hand, was a meat-and-potatoes man, and while he was away often, he still expected a hearty meal whenever he made it home for the night. We didn't always sit down as a complete family, but it was a goal and an expectation whenever everyone was home at mealtime. Fortunately, my girls helped to keep the house and to cook, and while the boys didn't always enjoy cleaning out animal pens in the barn, they were helpful just the same. Even with so many hands, there was always more to do.

We would preserve anything we could when the season was right. This allowed us to have fruits and vegetables without paying the big bucks during the winter. Whether fruit from our trees or vegetables from the garden, these places were sources of inexpensive and plentiful food that was essential to maintaining the family diet and our lean budget. With boys who loved to hunt, we would on rare occasions enjoy game—but most of my children had not inherited my childhood acceptance of such fare. We supplemented our fruits and veggies with at least some of our own eggs, farmed meat, and milk, but there was seldom so much that we were able to eliminate our weekly trips to the grocery store to secure a further twenty-two loaves of bread and seven pounds of butter.

Above: The complete White Family circa 1971

The family's appetite required a weekly grocery trip, which meant that every Saturday, we would pack up and head into town. Unlike today, we seldom topped up our supplies mid-week. It just wasn't done. Grocery shopping was always one and done for the week. This demanded careful planning and budgeting, and while it wasn't easy, we tried to turn this chore into a fun outing for the entire family.

I usually managed to hold back just enough money to treat us all to something special at the American Hotel. Clarence would head into the pool room, and the kids and I would head over to the little lunch counter where Mommy Baker would do up some hot and salty French fries and an ice-cold glass of bubbly ginger ale for each of the kids. If we were especially lucky that week, a stop at Maggie's for an ice cream cone was also in order.

It is entirely possible that the kids inherited their love for ice cream from me. I can still remember my own trips with my friend Kathleen into the ice cream shop in Brussels after Sunday services, so

I understood and even shared their excitement at the prospect of a stop at Maggie's. We made an entire day of the outing. This may not seem like much to people these days, but at the time, this was special, and the kids and I always looked forward to our Saturday afternoon trips into Brussels.

First on our to-do list was our weekly shopping stop for groceries at the Willis Bake Shop. In addition to all the necessary staples, like fresh bread, they sold certain specialty items like large blocks of cheddar cheese and sweet Chelsey buns by the bag. This bulk buying appealed to large families like ours. In addition to the items on our must-have list, Mr. Willis often slipped a few extras into my bags at no cost. This included the so-called day-olds that were still good but could no longer be sold to paying customers, as they were at the end of their shelf life and would not last another week (which would not be a problem at our hungry house). Sweet breads and other baked goods that were only slightly stale were a welcome and unexpected treat, so we appreciated his kind generosity.

We also appreciated his favourable payment terms. You see, much of what was sold at the Willis Bakery was sold in large quantities and for a fair price. Better still, Mr. Willis would take care of large local families by allowing us to pay when we could. At the time, it was not uncommon for some area businesses to permit locals to finance items in this way, as money was tight everywhere. I would sometimes buy essential items like food and even seasonal goods, like snowsuits, on this kind of a credit plan. Mr. Willis and a few other shops in town would let people he knew well pay in instalments. It was the only way we could get certain necessary items as they were needed.

In the case of the Willis Bake Shop, these favourable terms meant that almost without fail, we would stop in and grab a treat while we were in town. It was also quite common for Mr. Willis to make an unscheduled stop at our house as he was out making his regular deliveries through the week. He knew that, with a house full of hungry mouths to feed, extra bread would never go astray. If he was passing by the gate with a few unclaimed loaves in the truck, he would toss them onto our kitchen table and collect payment from us later. I must admit that an unexpected mid-week delivery of fresh bread was a wonderful find when I returned to the kitchen from the garden or from choring in the barn. I may have even been responsible for an occasional missing crust before the hungry gang came home from school.

Another favourite stop was a small butcher shop, owned by Mr. Baker, on the main street in Brussels. They stocked a kind of ring bologna that we called Baker's Bologna, and no trip to town was complete without first grabbing a chub of this indulgence. Usually at least one wiener for each of the children would not make it home, and the supply that did make it back to the farm didn't last long. With such a wonderful bounty, there was no cooking on Saturday nights at the White house. The kids and I would feast on bologna and fresh bread and plunk down for cartoons that always included the Road Runner.

Sometimes, we would wrap up our feast with a bowl of Kraft Dinner—one of the kids' most favourite treats. Occasionally, I would make up some rice pudding or even chocolate pudding, using my mother's recipe for chocolate syrup. Clarence would sometimes join us, but usually he would remain at the pool room to socialize and play darts at the Legion.

Once the younger children were settled and under the watchful eye of their older siblings, I would make a return trip for a night of darts with Clarence and friends. It's funny, but the kids still talk and laugh about these outings and simple pleasures when they gather together today. If I am being honest, my mouth still waters a little when I think of Baker's Bologna and fresh-made bread.

⌘

With such a big family, food was not the only thing that was in high demand. Space was also at a premium in the house. My three girls shared a room. That one wee room had a double bed and a cot, and there was a chalk line running across the floor between the two areas. Colleen claimed the cot, and her side of the room was always spic and span. The makeshift line was clearly delineated with a "Do Not Enter" sign because, while Colleen's tendency was to keep things in immaculate order, the other side of the line looked more like a hurricane had come ashore.

The mess didn't bother me much, but it drove Clarence wild. He always insisted that the beds should be made each morning before school. Susan didn't like to make her bed and often snuck away without completing the task, so to save us from war or divorce within the household, I started sneaking in and making her bed when they were away at school. This trick worked for a short while, but Clarence wasn't to be fooled for long. He really was a smart fella. Either that, or I am a terrible liar.

The kids were also smart—whip smart, in fact—but they still required careful supervision. More to the point, you couldn't leave them alone for a damn minute. It seemed like every time I turned my back or went out to the woodpile or garden, something went terribly wrong in the house. There was always some little drama at the White house.

Like the time when the kids were all sitting at the table with a sunflower. *What could it possibly hurt?* I foolishly thought. That was, until Brian stuffed a sunflower seed so far up his nose that we needed to see a doctor to have it removed. Keith was also known to swallow coins when we gave him change for a treat in town. I guess he didn't want anyone to get his money. At least he didn't lose it. I suppose he was the winner, because he ended up with some shiny-looking coins, although we didn't tell the store clerks where he had been keeping his change.

And it wasn't just the boys who found trouble. There was also the time that Colleen filled her nostrils with the fabric stuffing from one of her dolls. It took a lot of effort to hold her down long enough, but I eventually managed to get it all out with the tweezers. Crisis averted, and in time, she managed to calm down from the trauma of the entire experience. Never a dull moment at the White house.

While we enjoyed our Saturday trips to town, Sunday was a quieter day for us—or at least as quiet as a household of nine could ever be. Once we were all up, had finished our chores, and had eaten a hearty breakfast, we would often visit with friends or with our parents, or entertain friends who would stop by. In the early years, we didn't have a television, so morning cartoons—not that there was such a thing then—didn't form part of the regular household routine. Similarly rare was our regular weekly attendance at church. While we went when we could, Clarence was not especially a religious man, so church was not high up on his to-do list.

I did manage to wrestle him into a church to baptize the first five of our children. We dressed in our Sunday best, with Sid, Judy, Rick, Keith, and Colleen in tow, and headed off to the church. Clarence was never comfortable in a pew, and some car trouble on the way into town sealed our fate. That baptism was one of his final appearances at a regular Sunday service, although as he got older, he softened his hard stance and attended on occasions like family weddings.

Above: The White family of the day, in all our finery, getting the kids baptised at the Brussels church. It was a good day.

I am not sure why it stands out in my head, but we went the longest time without a refrigerator. We finally got one from Max Oldfield's Hardware in Brussels. Max trusted us to pay when we could, taking a few dollars here and there until the bill was paid up. I remember him making a note in his little book every time we made a payment. That is how he tracked his accounts. Thankfully, there were no credit checks, and I am not even sure there was interest required for him to hold the bill. I guess he wanted the business, and this was the only way to do it, because most folks didn't have the cash money to pay up front.

We got our first television in much the same way. It was sometime around 1955, and I was probably moaning about not having one because it seemed like everyone else was getting a TV. This would have sent Clarence over the edge, so off in the car he went, and it wasn't long before Max Oldfield delivered a new TV to the house and hooked it up, and we lurched into the modern age. We didn't get many channels at first—certainly there was no cable or satellite programming—but it was an amazing invention that quickly gained favour with the children.

I remember Sid, Judy, and to a lesser extent Rick being glued to that crazy box. You had to shoo them off the couch with a broom, they were so amazed. It was a great babysitter, and I used to joke that it paid for itself with peace and quiet alone. That old black-and-white TV may have been our first real luxury item.

At the time, some of these day-to-day happenings and events or missteps bothered me, but looking back, the sting is gone, and they now make me smile. For better or worse, it's like they are markers from a simpler time. I loved being a mom to seven little ones, even when times were lean—and believe me, times were often lean. We couldn't give the kids everything, but we managed to give them what they needed most. We didn't drive a fancy car or live in a large house, but the car and house we had were safe places where our family spent quality time and charted its course together.

Parenting today is so much more complicated and busier than in my day. I am not sure how people do it. I don't think kids are happier than they used to be. I am also not sure that parents take the time to enjoy their little ones when they are still little; it's a special time, and it all passes so quickly. If I can offer any advice to my own grandchildren, and eventually to my great-grandchildren, I would say to slow down and enjoy life. When it's over, it's over, and there is no going back. My experiences tell me that if you want your children to be happy and to turn out well, spend twice as much time and half as much money. Maybe that was the secret to our success. We had only time to spend.

CHAPTER 12

TIME FOR ME

*You are Never too Old to Set a New Goal or to
Dream a New Dream.*—C.S. Lewis

Clarence was always a good man, father, and husband; a great provider; and a hard worker at everything he did. But he was far from perfect. In fact, he was a stubborn perfectionist with a bark that was often far worse than his bite (but the bark was bad enough). Just like the rest of us, he had vices, and he made mistakes, but he was there for us when it mattered most.

Over the years, he took on many jobs, both on and off the farm, to make ends meet. This meant that he wasn't always present or what you might call hands-on with the children—which was par for the course for most men in those days. He was, however, there when and how we needed him most. I know that he set aside some of his own life goals and plans in favour of our shared needs, and I will always be grateful for his dedication to me and to our family.

The White house was never a place of great wealth. Like most of our friends and neighbours along the 5th Line, we worked hard and long for everything we ever had, but we did fine between Clarence's wages and what we were able to raise, scrounge, or save on our little homestead. Of course, things were not as luxurious as they are today, but we were genuinely happy, and we wanted for little. We always had good food on the table, a warm fire in the furnace, and a sound roof over our heads. We even had some nice extras when the occasion warranted. Things were just simpler all-around back then.

Clarence being away meant that I stayed at home to raise and care for the children for years. That was just the way of things in those days. In fact, from the time we were married until the 1980s, I tended to the farm, kept the house, and raised our children without really exploring my own interests. It was a good arrangement that worked well while the children were young and at home, but as they grew older and more independent—and one-by-one went off to school, and then on to lives and families of their own—I found that our little house got bigger and quieter than I was used to.

In response to the shifting demands at the White house, my social circle through the day slowly started to expand. Neighbour ladies like Mary Holmes, Althea and Isabelle Marks, and Mary Clark would stop by for coffee, conversation, and just to help pass the time together. We would set aside our chores and chatter away, set a perm, or just swap stories about the latest happenings up and down the concession. This was a nice diversion, but as more of the children headed out, I started looking beyond our gate.

To be clear, I certainly enjoyed my career as an active mother, but once the nest was nearly empty, I snapped up the opportunity to take on part-time jobs of my own. For the first time since I worked at the Blyth Hotel in the late 1940s, I was not just at home with the children. The newness of the experience was nice, but it took time to get used to. The extra money of my own was nice too, and I enjoyed having something to do through the day.

I started with odd jobs like painting and paper-hanging, and then moved my way up to things like housekeeping. Up until about the mid–1970s, I still needed to be home when the hungry children returned from school, so I needed to select jobs that allowed for that. On one occasion, Liz Sholdice, a long-time friend, and I agreed to pull and trim turnips for Bill Pease. Bill was a kind man who always treated us fairly, which we appreciated. He would often let us in to warm up with a coffee. We even took our lunch occasionally in where it was warm before heading back out to the field for the afternoon's work.

The job was quite physically demanding, but nothing that I wasn't used to. It was certainly far less physical than my time at the Libby's cannery in Chatham back in the days before I was married. It was also much easier than carrying around a couple of children when making dinner or sweeping the kitchen floor. It allowed flexible hours and decent pay mixed with the chance at some grown-up conversations.

⌒⌒⌒

After years of being at home with children, I discovered that I was a people person who very much enjoyed working with others. This realization led me to a twelve-year career as an Avon representative. My outgoing personality was a huge asset in this setting, and I excelled at sales. Best of all, the scheduling flexibility of door-to-door sales was a huge plus for a middle-aged woman just re-entering the workforce. I could set my own hours, take days off when one of the children was sick, or even work extra time or extra hours on weekends or in the evenings when my duties at home allowed for it.

Working for Avon was a great job by any measure. My sales were good, and in addition to the commission, social benefits, and other positive working conditions, Avon offered perks that excited me and opened doors to the world beyond the 5th Line. In particular, it turned out that Avon offered travel rewards for some of its best sellers. I hadn't travelled much in my youth, mostly because I came from a home of relatively modest means. That and the fact that our oldest son, Sid, arrived only a few weeks after my 19th birthday meant that I always had commitments other than taking far-flung holidays for most of my life. Aside from a summer vacation to the Argyle cottages in Goderich when I was a teenager and my summer away in southern Ontario for work, I had rarely been more than a few kilometres from home.

One year in particular, the trip being offered was a one-week, all-expense-paid vacation in the Bahamas. Imagine—a girl from the 5th Line of Morris Township jet-setting off to the tropics. As soon as I heard it, I set my sights on the big prize. I was determined to hit my sales thresholds and to make the cut for the free travel.

Word spread fast, and I was both pleased and surprised to see my sales number rise with each passing week. I had tremendous support from my regular customers, many of whom bought extra products to help bolster my sales tally that year. Everyone seemed excited to help me out. That was just the kind of neighbours we were lucky enough to have. Some had to buy on credit, but they were good people and I trusted them, so we made it work.

As the weeks rolled on, my sales grew, and eventually I hit my goal and qualified for a trip. For the first time, I was off alone in the big world on a wonderful adventure.

Above: As a top seller for Avon, I was treated to an all-expense-paid trip to the Bahamas. This was certainly as far from home as I had ever been. I truly had a grand time with the other ladies on the trip.

I packed a bag and said my goodbyes. I was picked up by a van in Brussels along with some of the other girls going on the trip. We were all quite excited to get underway. Once we were loaded, we started off to the airport. Our charter left Montreal, and after a short flight, we touched down in Nassau. A short overland trip later, and we were dipping our toes into the white sands along the Atlantic Ocean in front of our wonderful Paradise Island resort.

The entire week was the experience of a lifetime. Our rooms had private balconies overlooking the clear blue water. The stunning sunsets, the postcard-like scenery, and the endless food were like nothing I had ever seen. It was all truly amazing. We rode on boats, explored little craft shops, swam in the lagoon, and just took it all in. It may have been the first time I had ever seen a flamingo. They are so pretty.

We were given $35 per day to cover our lunch and expenses, so money was not a problem. Our evening meals were served in grand dining rooms, with shows to entertain us. That was the first time I'd ever tasted lobster.

They took care of every detail. For the first time, I had nothing in particular to do and no one else to worry about. I can still clearly remember the smell of the salt air and the sounds of the waves lapping against the shore when things got quiet at night. My travelling companions were balls of fun and helped the week to pass even faster than I could have imagined.

❦

Despite the fun, eventually my week by the sea was over, and I returned to Huron County. I enjoyed the week away, but there really is no place like home. I was glad to get back to my routine, but I certainly had lots of stories to tell—not that I ever had trouble finding stories to tell. The big take-away for me was that I had caught the travel bug, but I still had responsibilities at home, and we had a budget to keep. Trips would be less extravagant for a while, but we still managed to work some in.

For example, years later, some friends and I decided to take a few short-haul bus trips, just the girls. I was excited when we started the annual tradition of attending the Festival of Lights in Niagara Falls—the same place Clarence and I had taken our ill-timed winter honeymoon—to take in the sights and the shows.

Above: I always enjoyed our ladies' weekend away at the Festival of Lights in Niagara Falls. Those were good times with good friends. We were into Christmas sweaters long before they were trendy.

I can say that Niagara Falls is a far nicer place to visit when the streets are not packed with snow and slush. Those were fun days that make me smile whenever I think about them. I certainly enjoyed travelling with the girls, but I especially enjoyed when Clarence joined in on the fun. There was the time in the summer of 1989 when Clarence and I took a car trip to the East Coast of Canada with our friends Jack and Ruth Pipe. We had so much fun that time. I always wanted to go there again but just never found the time.

We did have the chance to go to Florida twice with our friends Fanny and George Somers. It was always great to get away, and best of all, to really start enjoying some recreation together as a couple, away from all the work and bustle of our regular life. At the time, I certainly felt that we had earned it.

Above: Jack and Ruth Pipe, Clarence, and I, during our summer drive to Canada's East Coast in 1989. The Reversing Falls are rapids on the Saint John River located in Saint John, New Brunswick, near the Bay of Fundy.

Now, I wouldn't want to leave the impression that we did nothing fun at all together until all the kids were gone. In fact, Clarence was always quite spontaneous—sometimes to a fault. He liked to travel when the mood struck him.

I remember one Friday night when Clarence came home from playing darts at the Legion. We were just sitting at the table when he blurted out, "I think I'll go west." It turned out that he had been talking to his pal Leonard at the Legion, and they had hatched a plan to drive out west for two weeks. I quickly learned that we were scheduled to leave two days later on Monday morning. I protested the tight departure timelines, questioned the budget, and even tried pointing out that it would be impossible to find a sitter for six children for two weeks. But his mind was made up, and Clarence would hear none of it. In his gruffest voice, he declared, "We're going, so you'll just need to figure it out."

I later found out that he had planned to sell two cattle from the barn to finance the excursion and was expecting that my mother would watch the kids while we were away. It was the summer of 1965, just a few months before our youngest son, Brian, was born, so my mother was shocked and more than a little concerned to learn of our sudden and ambitious plan to drive more than five thousand miles round trip. She feared that so much time in the bumpy, hot, and dusty car—we took our old two-door Mercury Comet, and there was no such thing as air conditioning in those days—would cost us the baby. Despite her concerns, she agreed to watch the children.

Leonard and his wife, Jean (who was also my cousin), and Clarence and I ended up leaving on the Tuesday morning, and we drove all the way to Vancouver, British Columbia. I remember that I was worried about the kids the entire time we were away. I sent a never-ending stream of postcards back to them, and as much as the trip was interesting, I missed them terribly. Despite the fact that I usually liked travelling and seeing new sights, I am glad that our longer trips happened after the children were a wee bit older.

❦

Travel aside, this was also a time when Clarence and I started the journey toward being empty nesters—or at the very least, parents without toddlers in the house. Until then, my life had revolved around the children, keeping our home, and making sure that our farm was running when Clarence was at work or otherwise away. Looking back, I really had nothing to complain about. I always looked at this as my duty as a wife and mother. It may not be the modern way, but it was the way of things at the time, and I wouldn't change a thing if I could.

In those days, we kept a market garden at home, as vegetables were essential to keeping our balanced diet and tight budget when the children were younger, and they were equally a source of extra cash once there were fewer mouths to feed in later years. I always enjoyed gardening and plants in general. Perhaps that was one of my passions. Equally passionate was Clarence and his desire for perfection (perhaps this explains why he married me), which created a need for our garden to be 100 per cent weed-free at all times. We also grew garlic, which

130

is a crop that demands lots of time working on your hands and knees just to grow it. It is back-breaking work, but we did it.

Above: Clarence surveys the field. Not a weed in sight.

After years of apprenticeship training on our own farm, I decided to pursue my plant passion in a direction that didn't involve gardening or farming. Now that I had some time to do things purely for fun, I joined up with the Brussels Horticultural Society, and in time, I even served as president of the club for a few years. This local group of budding horticulture and gardening enthusiasts may have been one of the first clubs that I ever joined, and I did it because I thought it would be fun. It was fun, but it was also a learning experience.

The club participated in parades, maintained the Brussels Horticultural Park and planters, worked at the Butterfly Garden, and just enjoyed each other's company while growing our love of plants and gardening. In 1994, after taking a judging course in London, I was awarded certification from the Ontario Horticultural Association as an official judge, which further encouraged me to get involved in the community and to more aggressively pursue interests that were mine and mine alone.

Above: The ceremony where I was awarded my credentials as a judge with the Ontario Horticultural Association. Below: My Ontario Horticultural Association Judging Certificate. After my lengthy apprenticeship in our own gardens on the farm, I took my expertise on the road.

Horticultural Judging Certificate

This is to certify that

JANE WHITE

has successfully completed the School of Judging and Exhibiting, comprising courses on flowers, fruits, vegetables and floral design;
coordinated by the
Ontario Horticultural Association
Ontario Agriculture Societies
Ontario Ministry of Agriculture and Food

Dated this 28TH day of JUNE 19 96.

Pauline Richards
Course Coordinator

Becoming a horticulture judge introduced me to the idea that I had real skills and knowledge to share with others. As a child, I had used my cleverness to gain advantages for myself—to get out of chores I disliked or to skip out on classes. Then, in later years, I used my smarts to raise my children and to keep the house and farm running smoothly. As a judge, I would be responsible and even expected to critique the hard work and personal efforts of strangers and of those outside of my own household. It was new territory, but I was eager for the challenge.

If I am being honest, it wasn't until years later that I even considered the significance of the change. You never really think about these things when they're happening because it's just the way it was. The truth is that I had happily spent my entire adult life working to care for others and provide for their wants and needs, but as the children grew and started to move on, I took the opportunity to move on too. I knew how to work, and I wasn't afraid to venture out on a limb.

With my formative steps into the job market, and eventually joining clubs and honing new skills, I began to explore my own interests and to take on hobbies that would introduce me to new friends and activities that would help to shape the person I would become. Today, it is hard to imagine a time before these things, because they came to be so important to me.

Above: In September of 1987, Shirley Wheeler, Ruth Sauve, Alf Knight, and I wave and smile from the Horticultural Society's float in the Brussels parade.

My granddaughters Michelle McNichol and Shannon White joined me on the float as our little flower girls.

The Horticulture Society may have been one of my first interests outside of my own home and aside from my children, but it was not to be the last. I had an energetic personality, a great sense of humour, a green thumb, and a sunny sky ahead of me.

Chapter 13

The Pot of Gold

If children are the rainbow of life.
Grandchildren are the pot of gold.
—An Old Saying

As the children grew, I took on more and more responsibilities outside of our home and apart from our own family. Eventually, this included a progression away from part-time field work and casual paper-hanging to more conventional full-time work. My first full-time regular job was a stint as a housekeeper at Calendar's, the nursing home in Brussels at the time. The owner, Mr. MacGowan, also owned a facility in Wingham where I would later work once the Brussels location closed.

Now, I didn't have a fancy degree or years of schooling to back me up, but I knew how to work, and that still mattered. The world then was not so focused on paper credentials as it is today. In fact, I suspect my years keeping house and raising children made me just the kind of person they were looking for. The place had the feel of a big family all living under one roof, and I was certainly familiar with that vibe. It was the type of place where everyone happily celebrated everyone's birthday with cupcakes and a song. I knew all the residents and really enjoyed chatting and visiting with everyone in the place. We took care of each other, which made it a fun place to be whether you were an employee or a resident.

I made lots of great friends, and I worked there—and eventually at the Wingham location—until I was sixty-five, when I made the decision to retire. The facility had changed ownership by then. It was known as Braemar, but other than the sign over the doors, little had changed since I had started. On my last day, there were hugs, flowers, and even some tears as I left the building one last time and started yet another chapter in my life.

Above: My final day of work at the nursing home in Wingham. I enjoyed the work and made good friends, but post-retirement, I focused on being a grandmother.

I suppose all of this happened gradually, as it was less and less necessary for me to be home when the children returned from school each day. This is not to suggest that our children were latchkey kids, just to say that as they got older, they were more independent and required far less parental supervision. Some had even left for their own lives and families by this time.

Brian was the last to leave home—in 1984, when he was eighteen—but by that time, Sid was already in his early thirties and married. Likewise, Judy and Colleen had married off and started families of their own, and so on. One by one, my babies had babies, and I got to wear a new title: grandma. I really enjoyed it.

⌘

The year 1984 was also when my life hit another serious bump in the road, something that again changed me forever. It was that summer when I lost my mother.

My mother was a fun, smart, and amazing woman in her own right, and she was also a caring and devoted wife and mother who taught me so much. She didn't always fully appreciate her own abilities or how important she was to us, but she worked hard every day to give Daddy, Tony, and I a loving and safe place in the world—and she did it all with the talents God gave her.

She was a tremendous cook who made much from nothing. I still remember buzzing around at her heels in the kitchen at home, bombarded by such wonderful smells and watching as she made meals from thin air that I still remember as mouth-watering. Thick-sliced warm bread with freshly churned butter (from the butter churn she loved so much), rich homemade chocolate syrup poured into creamy milk from our own cows, and fruity Jell-O—I always loved Jell-O—and she wasted absolutely nothing as she did it all.

I even remember her making me a wonderful borg coat. I was the height of fashion when I put that on. We used to joke that she could actually stretch a tin of salmon, because she could make an entire platter of sandwiches from a single can.

It was a good thing she was so able in the kitchen, because she and Daddy were ever the willing and generous hosts. My mother was a giving woman who was always kind to family, neighbours, and strangers alike. Her generosity was as endless as her energy. No matter how little we had, she seemed perfectly content and even happy having nothing other than her friends and family around—and she was especially fond of her grandchildren.

My mother loved having our children in her house, and they loved visiting with her. Part of it was just the company, but I suspect there was also a lot of spoiling that happened when visiting with Grandma

Ovington. For example, when the children were over during the summer, she would often send them to the store to pick up a brick of ice cream and a bottle of ginger ale. When they returned to the house, ice cream floats were on the menu for all. If that's not spoiling, I am not sure what is.

Aside from her love of entertaining, her personal strength, and the frugality of her smartly stashing away tins of salmon so my brother, Tony, wouldn't eat them (just in case she needed them for a surprise guest; we found several cans of salmon stashed away in her house after she died), my mother was a bit of a character. She was quite superstitious and often devoted a portion of her fifteen dollars weekly salary to visiting a fortune teller. She also learned to read tea leaves for friends and relatives—a skill she was all too keen to pass on. While it has been years since I partook, as I remember, we would all sit and chat over a cup of tea in a proper china cup and saucer. Once we all had emptied our cups, we needed to rotate the cup three times on the saucer and then turn it upside-down. Then the reading would happen, followed by yet more conversation, socializing, and tea.

Readings like this never revealed heavy subjects of tragedy, but she would predict incoming packages or long trips away. In 1965, she predicted a road trip west that Clarence and I would take with his friend Leonard and Leonard's wife, Jean. Some believed—like Cousin Jean—while others like me just enjoyed the outing.

Either way, I have many wonderful memories of my mother, and I credit her for helping to make me into the person I am today. She was good to Daddy, Tony, and me; she was good to my children; and we all loved her dearly. July 5, 1984, was a sad day for all of us.

⌘

As with all things, the sad summer of 1984 eventually gave way to brighter days. For example, our first grandson was born in the spring of 1976 (James Eldon McNichol), and in the years that followed, that number swelled to 15 grandchildren (plus their eventual spouses) and 23 great-grandchildren. In fact, our most recent great-granddaughter (Delaney Clair White) was born on October 9, 2020, as this book was being written, and I hear another arrival is scheduled before we go to print.

As someone with considerable experience in these matters, let me tell you that grandchildren are your opportunity to do some things over again. As with many grandparents, Clarence and I were in quite a different place in our lives. Money and time weren't as scarce as when we were younger, so we had the opportunity to grandparent much differently than we had parented.

Not everything had changed, though. Just as I was with my own children, I enjoyed being hands-on and present for the grandkids—and not just when they were little. I always enjoyed watching school plays, having them for sleepovers at the farm, and even just watching them play together in the field. Nothing made me happier than blocks and toy tractors scattered over the floor, or lots of little voices and laughter around the farm again.

Suddenly, our White Christmas gathering and the annual Father's Day get-together took on a fun new energy. Little ones will do that. They change the feel and add something new and special, and as grandparents, you get to give them homemade oatmeal cookies whenever you want and then send them home for Mom and Dad to deal with when the sugar hits. It really is the best of all things.

As some of our grandchildren grew older, we have had the privilege of enjoying time with them as children, teens, and then as adults. Like the time we travelled to Ireland to meet my cousins with our daughter Judy; her husband, Ross; and their two children, Scott and Heather. It was a wonderful experience seeing Scott and Heather enjoying themselves on their first big international trip.

I remember that Clarence nearly had a fit with Scott every time we went into a hotel room for the night. Scott was a curious wee boy, pushing every button and pulling every lever at every opportunity. Clarence was worried that Scott was going to break something, so he worked endlessly to keep ahead of the energetic youngster. The kids were good and travelled well, and in the end, we really enjoyed the trip. Clarence just needed to learn to go with the flow—something he never really excelled at.

There was also the time when Clarence and I visited our granddaughter Julie and her husband at their home in Ottawa. As I remember it, we opted to jump in their car at the last second to join them on their return drive home to Ottawa. In our haste to get ready for a snap departure, Clarence left his wallet and all his money at home on the dresser. This was something he only realized after announcing that he would buy lunch for everyone at our first stop.

His irritation with his own forgetfulness seemed to lessen somewhat when we noticed that I had forgotten half of my own suitcase—including my pajamas. We managed to still have a good trip, but there was an awful lot of laughing and teasing over our forgotten essentials. This included some chiding from our local Member of Parliament, who playfully reminded me that "Pajamas are only good for hanging on the bedpost in case of fire."

Above: I remind everyone that I am in charge during a visit to Parliament in Ottawa. The Speaker's Chair is quite different from the chairs around our kitchen table, but I managed to make it work.

Before all the grandchildren appeared on the scene, and before I retired, Clarence and I enjoyed our new life as empty nesters. We were both still busy at work, but we enjoyed social time with each other and with our friends whenever we could. When the children were small, we seldom got out to parties like we had when we were in our teens. We played darts at the Brussels Legion and cards with the neighbours. Clarence was quite good, and I enjoyed outings to places like Blyth, where we went most Friday nights for darts, or Brussels, where we played darts each Saturday night. We even attended the odd kitchen party up and down the line, but otherwise, we stayed close to home.

Once the children were gone, we often took friends for sightseeing drives. Clarence was a great one to drive all over the country. Our trips typically included some light shopping, lots of laughter, a meal out, and then the journey home. Every fall, we went away down near Chatham for a couple of days and filled the car with fresh field-grown tomatoes that we picked ourselves. There is nothing quite like the taste of a fresh field tomato. They are so much better than a grocery store or hothouse tomato. They were always a bit cheaper that way too, and we were never shy about getting a good deal when we could. We would take them home, and I would spend the days following our trip processing and canning our pickings for the following winter. Even without so many mouths to feed, we still did this kind of work. I guess old habits die hard.

Clarence also took to grilling, so we started to have barbecues with neighbours, family, and friends. The freezer was always full of hamburgers from Green's Meats and buns just in case we had an unexpected visitor stop in at mealtime. It became quite normal for us to host outdoor meals of sausage, hot dogs, or hamburgers on a Saturday or Sunday afternoon. In fact, somewhere along the line, we started a Father's Day steak barbecue tradition where all the kids and their families would come home for the day.

There was also the May work bee. I think that one started when the kids figured we were getting too old to do some jobs on our own, so they all came over and did painting, digging flower beds, and finishing up other odd jobs to help us out. We would all spend the day working and playing games, and then wrap it up with a cold beer and meal together. We continued this tradition for as long as we lived on our little five-acre farm.

Above: Clarence takes to the grill at our annual Father's Day barbecue.

This was also a time when I resumed another old hobby that I quite enjoyed. In my younger days, I always kept a sewing machine on hand. I made clothes and winter mittens for the children (and eventually for my grandchildren and great-grandchildren) and mended what we had to extend the useful life of socks, pants, shirts, and the like. Eventually, I started to make quilts. At first, I made them because we needed the bedding, but then I started making more decorative patterns and gifting the quilts.

At this point, I have made at least one nice quilt for each of my children, grandchildren, and great-grandchildren. I also have a few in my own home. At first, I hand-quilted them, but today, as arthritis has set into my fingers, I have been forced to resort to tied quilts. They are still quite nice, and I still need to cut up the blocks and assemble them, but it is much easier on my fingers.

Above: I belonged to the Five Star Quilting Guild for several years. Here is one of my many quilting creations. This one is the Irish Chain pattern.

While I am not sure how much longer I will be able to make quilts, I plan to keep trying right to the end. I really enjoy it, and it helps me to pass the time on those cold winter nights alone at home.

~~~

But life wasn't all card parties and quilting bees. I should mention one of our other great hobbies, one that Clarence and I did together. For many years, we liked to gamble. I suppose it was social for us too. Whether stopping in to play the slots at the casino during our road trips to Niagara Falls or Clinton, buying scratch tickets, or trying our luck in the Lottario draw and then watching patiently for the winning numbers after the evening news, Clarence and I enjoyed playing the odds. Of course, we were careful not to over-indulge or risk too much. Clarence could have a bit of an addictive personality at times, so he was always quite careful.

Clarence, who was also as stubborn as a mule, tracked our winnings and our losses meticulously. We typically used our winnings to finance our playing, and we never counted on the money as income or to pay bills. I guess you could say we looked at our gambling activities as recreation. Just like some might go out to a movie and spend twenty dollars for the night, Clarence and I would do the same at the casino, and if we came home with some extra jingle in our pockets, then so be it. We had fun either way.

On more than one occasion, we won respectable jackpots. For example, we once won a $9,800 purse in the Owen Sound Legion's 50/50 draw. As I remember, Clarence bought the ticket from a work friend on a bit of a lark. We had as much fun dreaming about winning as we did once we won. At least before actually winning, we could talk of grand trips and other extravagances, whereas once we won, we opted for a new refrigerator, a TV, and some other household necessities.

There was also the time we won $9,000 in the Lottario draw. The entire affair was quite exciting, but we needed to drive to Toronto to collect our winnings, which came in the form of a cheque presentation and a photo op. Our daughter Susan and her eventual husband, Carl Bondi, joined us on the trip. What a day that was—you can't usually buy that much fun for a dollar. This time, we used the winnings for a trip to the east coast of Canada. It was time to reward ourselves.

Above: Hauling down the big bucks in the lottery— here we gather our $9,000 winnings from the Lottery Corporation in Toronto. Our daughter Susan and her future husband, Carl Bondi, join in the fun.

As the years passed, our trips to the casino seemed to lessen, until one day, they stopped entirely. I am not sure why, but just as the card parties started to fade, so too did our bus trips and casino ventures. They helped us to pass the time, to meet and enjoy the company of friends, and to revisit some of the fun and excitement that Clarence and I had first encountered in our youth at those old community dances in the township hall. I guess we just outlived the experience and moved on to other things. I sure am glad we made those wonderful memories when we did, because they still make me smile when I think about all the fun we had.

CHAPTER 14

SAYING GOODBYE

Death leaves a heartache no one can heal,
love leaves a memory no one can steal.
—Inscribed on an Irish Headstone

In September of 2012, after nearly 50 years on the farm, Clarence and I said goodbye to our neighbours on the 5th Line of Morris Township (now Huron County Road 16 or Morris Road), and we unpacked our personal belongings and family treasures in our new home near the north end of Wingham. I was sad to leave our small country house and the old neighbourhood that had been our home from the beginning, but it was time to go. We started to find that certain tasks and routine jobs that were once easy for us had been getting harder and harder. Keeping the grass and the yard to Clarence's high standard was almost impossible, even though we no longer kept a garden. The steps were getting longer, and my legs were not the dancing legs they once were.

The winters that had always challenged us with their cold and harsh winds continued, only now it was growing harder for us to stay ahead of the snow as it piled up in the lane. Our relative isolation, especially through winter storms, worried the kids. So, after many difficult conversations, Clarence and I decided that it was time to find a new place to put down roots and build memories.

I loved our farm. I had always lived on that very road. I found it hard to imagine that any other place could feel so much like home. Our house was always a busy place that we packed with as many people as we could fit. There was always room for one more visitor or member of the family at the kitchen table for a meal. I hated the thought that anyone would ever leave hungry, so I was ever ready to put on a spread of some kind, at the drop of a hat. Like my mother before me, I saw food as the root of hospitality. People were always stopping in on us, and that is just how I liked it. In many ways, the household that Clarence and I had built featured the hospitable and open-door policy that my parents had insisted on all those years ago.

Above: Our kitchen table at home always had room for more people. Here, several of my grandchildren and great-grandchildren crowd around to enjoy each other's company for Christmas 2005. In the background, you can see the kitchen cabinets that Clarence built for me.

When the time came, we packed our things and our memories, looked around our old home, and closed the door one last time. We headed just a few miles west to the town of Wingham—the place where we had watched Roy Rogers movies in our younger days. Our two-bedroom row house is new, modern, and much smaller than our previous home. It didn't have the knotty-pine woodwork or the cupboards that Clarence had hand-crafted and painstakingly fitted into my kitchen on the farm, nor did it have the view out onto the fields, but it was to be our home.

I was so happy that we managed to find a space for the four-piece glass-and-wood china cabinets that Clarence had made for me. It would have killed me to leave them behind. I guess bringing them with us to Wingham let me keep a little piece of our old home.

Once we were unpacked, we started to explore our new community and our new neighbours—but not before properly saying goodbye to our neighbours and friends from the farm. Wayne Fear and his wife, Barb, hosted a wonderful neighbourhood party for us, and everybody came. It was so nice to have one last blast with the crew who had been such an important part of our lives for so long.

Truthfully, the old gang was breaking up, as many of our concession neighbours were facing the same difficult dilemma we were. Downsizing and moving into town is just something that people tend to deal with as they get a little older, and we needed to face it like any other challenge that had popped up over the years. We were only moving a few miles away to Wingham, but leaving the neighbourhood meant that things would change. Of course, change was something that had always been part of our life together.

Above: After forty-nine years on the farm and a lifetime living on the 5ᵗʰ Line, Clarence and I enjoyed a going-away party hosted by our neighbours. We were not moving far, but lots would change.

We would stay in touch with our old friends, and we would even visit when we could. Fortunately, we were lucky to also find new neighbours who were friendly and helpful, and who quickly grew to be close friends. We soon discovered that living in town was actually a nice deal. Things were much more convenient. It was easier to get groceries in the winter; amenities were closer; and while our house was smaller, it was no less a little community than we were used to.

Getting to the doctor, dentist, and hairdresser was also much easier, and that was important because as we got older, we seemed to have more parts that needed regular attention and upkeep. I guess I am like an old car, and my parts are wearing out. I sometimes wonder which will last longer: me or the car. In any event, we quickly settled into our life in Wingham.

We started to become regulars for coffee at the local Tim Horton's with a klatch of area residents. We spent loads of time sitting on our new neighbours' decks—and they on ours—visiting, laughing, and solving all the problems of the world. It was and is quite normal for one of us to bake a pie or some other treat and to then share it with all the others.

The vast distance between houses had made this kind of interaction a little harder on the farm, so I enjoyed being closer now. Most importantly, those drop-in visits that I'd always enjoyed so much kept happening, but now, as there was no need for work bees, we could just visit. (This proximity and the intimate nature of our neighbourhood was always nice but proved even more useful when the COVID-19 global pandemic came knocking in early 2020.)

This all seemed grand, but we quickly realized that space was at a premium, so our annual Father's Day barbecue and events like the White Christmas needed to find new venues if the traditions were going to continue. Luckily, the children stepped up. The large Christmas, birthday, and Easter gatherings continued, but now they were at Colleen and Murray's, Keith and Jayne's, or Ross and Judy's place, and I just had to show up and enjoy myself as new traditions took root and the extended White family continued to grow.

Above: The parties and family gatherings continued, only now I just had to show up and enjoy as new traditions took root. Here we celebrate the birthday of a great-grandchild at Colleen's house. Below: My dream of a White Christmas continued, even after we no longer had the space to host.

All in all, life in Wingham was far better than we had dared to imagine. That was, until one terrible evening in August of 2014.

A little more than a year after we moved to town, Clarence's health started to falter. It started small at first, but things became more difficult as time passed. One night, he slipped on the tile floor and hurt himself badly. Some of the kids and the ambulance came, and we all headed off to the hospital. Sadly, after a short stay, it became clear that Clarence's health was far worse than we expected. In fact, things were so bad that we lost him just days later, on August 15, 2014.

The next morning, for the first time in almost seventy-five years, I woke up in a world without Clarence, and there was an empty space in my house and in my heart. We had been married for 65 years but had known each other our entire lives. We first met when I was just a little girl puddling in the river with my dog, and it seemed like only yesterday that we had attended SS No. 3. I could clearly remember the times we made the trip into town to watch Roy Rogers and Trigger on the big screen, and it didn't seem like so long ago—but it was.

Above: Clarence and I always enjoyed a good party. I still think about the times when we danced the night away.

It was quite a shock to see it all end. I spent that first day, and many days since, looking back and remembering our times together. Our earliest days were some of the best and most carefree of our entire lives.

Sure, we had many good and memorable times in our more than seven decades together—raising children and spending time with friends and family—but those early days were the days when we first fell in love. That was when we got to know each other best.

I will never forget our time together, and I will always be grateful for those years we had. Things were not always easy—Clarence was sometimes stubborn and set in his ways—but he was a good man, husband, father, and grandfather. He always provided for us, and we all succeeded because of his hard work and commitment to me and to our children.

Even after all the time had passed, he was my first and my only love, and I miss him and remember him always.

CHAPTER 15

PARTY OF ONE

*You cannot be lonely if you like the person
you're alone with.*—*Wayne Dyer*

It has been more than seven years since Clarence left, and while I miss
him terribly each day, life since then has been both different and good.
I keep busy, but not as busy as in my younger days. I visit with friends
and family whenever I can, and I try new things if possible.

In the last few years, I have learned how to live by myself, cooking
for one, for the first time in my life. I have tried my hand at senior's tai
chi, danced to Charlie Pride's "Crystal Chandelier" at my granddaughter
Jenni's wedding, took a ride in a big white limousine, and attended a
Blue Jays game in Toronto. Who would have imagined such things in
my future?

Above: You are never too old to try new things. Here I show off my tai chi abilities with some friends.

I remember my Blue Jays experience particularly well and with great fondness. We were all at an Easter gathering at my son Keith's house when the conversation turned to my long-time love of baseball. I had just mentioned to my granddaughter Julie that I enjoyed watching the ball game—especially when my team was on the field—when someone suggested that we should see a game live. I immediately resisted the idea, because I sometimes have trouble walking long distances over uneven ground, so I figured the stadium was really not the place for me.

My daughter Susan and her husband, Carl, who have been to many games at many stadiums, insisted that this was not a problem. The next thing I knew, a date was set, and an entire plan was in motion. May 21, 2018, was the day we headed for the ballpark in Toronto.

I spent the night before the big game at Carl and Susan's house in New Hamburg. Colleen had been kind enough to drop me off the day before so I wouldn't be too tired from travelling the day of the game. We were joined the next morning by my granddaughter Julie and her family. We chatted for a bit and started to get ready to go when I noticed a big white limousine pull up in front of the house. It was white and shiny, and it didn't look like a hearse at all. I was so excited. For the first time in my life, I was in a limousine. We were riding in style.

We all posed for pictures and then loaded into the beautiful car. The road trip to the park was loads of fun. We enjoyed some snacks and a nip or two of something called *mimosas*. My great-grandson Koby even introduced me to a pastry called a Pop-Tart. I had never had any of these things, but I was ready to try anything. I was learning so much, and we hadn't even gotten out of the car yet.

Once we arrived at the park, the big car pulled around to a special entrance, and a Blue Jays staff person was there waiting with a wheelchair. There were more pictures, and then I was whisked away to my VIP seats for the game. The entire experience was so exciting, and the game hadn't even started yet. We grabbed huge beers and took up our positions to watch the game. The game was fantastic, but I think I spent most of the day laughing and looking around at the stadium.

When it was all over, the Blue Jays had lost, but I didn't even care. We headed back to our car, but not before a policeman presented me with a game-used baseball. There were more pictures and more laughs. It was a grand day.

Above: A grand day at the ball game with my family—something I didn't think was still possible but something I will always remember.

Not every day is as exciting as all that, though. These days, I stay relatively close to home except for some day trips to places like Bright, where an area family puts on a meal and a wonderful musical performance. It is always a nice outing. I also enjoy going for drives with my neighbours and friends—people like Hugh and Georgina. We never struggle for conversation, and the days always pass quickly. These are just day trips, because I don't care for night driving anymore. I like the travel and the scenery, but I just prefer the daytime to be on the road if I'm the one driving.

Just like at home with Daddy, my mother, and Tony when I was a little girl, I still enjoy an occasional game of crokinole with friends or neighbours. It is a nice way to pass the time. The terrible arthritis in my fingers means I need a crokinole stick to make my shots, but I can still get the job done. I am more interested in the conversations than the score, but the game is still part of it all.

Porch parties are also a great way to pass the time in our little community. There are some truly nice people in my row, and I have enjoyed getting to know them. It is nice to be part of the group and to know that you have a support network so close at hand. We always have lots to chat and laugh about, and we often share some treats like pie or cookies that we have baked. After all, it is far nicer cooking for more than one.

I like being on the porch anyway, enjoying the sun, watching the birds at the feeders Clarence put up, or even making pets out of some of the local wildlife (just like when I was little). It somehow takes me back to my days dashing through the field and into the bush behind Daddy's farm on the 5th Line. For a while, I had adopted a squirrel that would come and take peanuts from my fingers. I even found him helping himself once from the peanut can just inside the patio door when I forgot to pull the door closed. I named the bold little critter Chipper, but I don't see him around anymore. I guess he is off doing squirrel stuff somewhere else.

Other than that, I pass the time with my puzzles, quilting, or even by baking my special oatmeal cookies that some of the grandchildren seem to enjoy so much. I stay connected with my extended family in Ireland and talk on the phone to my children, grandchildren, and friends near and far as much as I can. I look forward to family gatherings, but for now, the pandemic has put all that on hold, so my travels are confined largely to my mind as I read the pages of a good book from my living room rocker. I like to read novels. I like something that has a bit of a story to it. Reading was not something that I did much of when I was a little girl, but I have come to quite enjoy it these days.

I also enjoy spending time at my daughter Colleen's cottage north of Goderich. It is a lovely little place overlooking Lake Huron that I very much like to visit. On occasion, I even spend the night in the cozy and quiet little getaway. When I do, I especially enjoy watching the sunsets from the bluff overlooking the lake. The colours are amazing, and the entire place is peaceful and pretty. It is one of my favourite places. In fact, that is where the first few pages of this book were written.

ﾟ

All in all, for the most part, both my family and I have been healthy and happy, although late last November (2020), we suffered a terrible loss. My grandson Kevin (Keith's son) lost his dear wife, Elizabeth, after a battle with cancer. It was really the first loss, aside from Clarence in 2014, that the White family had been forced to endure in many years. It was awful. Elizabeth was just forty years old, and she left behind three wonderful little boys (Nicholas, Lucas, and Mitchell). COVID-19 meant that we could not all be with her right at the end, but I still think of her. That first Christmas was already hard enough with social distancing measures and all. An empty chair at our socially distant family table made things even harder and again reminded me of how important family is in the good times and especially in the bad.

All this said, the past few years on my own have been challenging, amazing, and unique. I have recovered well from some heart troubles a few years back, and aside from the arthritis in my fingers, I enjoy pretty good health. It does not take as much to fill my time as it once did, but I still enjoy doing new and fun things. Luckily, I never seem short on things to do (like writing a book).

In particular, I enjoy when people stop in for a visit. I suppose this is nothing new for me. I have always enjoyed the company of others and sharing the hospitality of my home. This is something I learned at a young age from my parents. The only difference today is that with age and hopefully wisdom, I have come to appreciate that the world is a busy and uncertain place, which has caused me to truly value time spent with family and good friends.

When I was at home on the farm, tending to the children, helping with chores, pursuing my hobbies, or even working out, it was always easy to get caught up in the hustle and bustle of day-to-day tasks. Now I have come to a point in my life when I look forward to a good book, a great sunset, or an unexpected visit from a loved one.

Above: Always my own person and ready for whatever life throws my way

CHAPTER 16

THE BEST IS YET TO COME

May you have the hindsight to know where you've been.
The foresight to know where you're going.
And the insight to know when you're going too far.
—An Irish Blessing

As I worked on this book, recalling people, places, and stories from my past, I looked out my living room window and thought about where I am now and how I came to be here. The road has been long, winding, and sometimes a little bumpy, but the place I have finally landed is one that makes me happy. These days are certainly interesting, and they seem to lend themselves quite well to reminiscing about the past—warts and all. There was a time when I imagined that the world of a hundred years ago must have looked quite different for Daddy and his family. Today, after looking more carefully at the happenings of even the past few years, I have come to believe that there may be more similarities than I first thought.

At this moment, I have plenty of time to think about these things, as the world is shut-in because of the COVID-19 virus that is cutting its way through our communities. I have had my vaccination, but since March of 2020, we have been largely confined to our homes as we watched on the news as our case numbers grew and in turn sparked fierce discussion and debate around every table.

Our world has changed because of this pandemic. In some ways, COVID-19 has helped us to remember and to refocus on what is most important by winding back the clock to a much simpler time. It has been interesting and even hard, but it is history in the making. We have spent more time chatting on the phone and less time racing about in the car. We even opted not to have our big White Family Christmas in person in 2020, opting instead for a high-tech Zoom computer call with children, grandchildren, and great-grandchildren. It seems you *can* teach an old dog new tricks.

It was in that context that I opted to write this book as a personal remembrance of how things were, and how lucky we are. We live in interesting times, but we have much to be thankful for. For me, I have relatively good health; my children are grown and happy; and I have come to know each of my fifteen grandchildren and twenty-three great-grandchildren (and counting). Life is grand.

Above: Clarence and I stand on the side lawn of our home farm in Morris-Turnberry (the White house) with our children and their spouses in 2009. Left to right—Sid and Melody, Rick and Debbie, Brian and Cathy, Susan and Carl, Jane and Clarence, Colleen and Murray, Judy and Ross, and Keith and Jayne.

Who could have imagined that the rough-and-tumble wee girl from the 5th Line of Morris Township, with roots deep in Wicklow, Ireland, would eventually find her way to Wingham, Ontario, with such a wonderful crew? As I think back all those years to Daddy alone on that ship, as he was sailing away from his home and parents, I wonder if this is a future he dared to dream of. I know for sure that, as a little girl splashing through the muddy Maitland River near my home, I never thought I could have it this good.

Of course, things have not always been easy, but I think my positive attitude and my mischievous sense of humour have kept me grounded and put me in good stead for whatever came my way in life. Good friends and a close family filled in the blanks from there. Perhaps there is a lesson to be learned somewhere here?

To my children and family, including the branches on the tree that have yet to appear, this book is my gift to you. I hope it brings you a smile, and I hope you find a pearl of wisdom or two between its covers. This book is a selective and condensed version of my nearly ninety years of living, but with any luck I will get to add a few more pages and chapters in the years ahead. In the meantime, my greatest wish for each of you is that you live long and healthy lives, filled with interesting times, good friends, and lots of people to love.

Above: My man Clarence and I walk together, hand-in-hand, along the lane to our home (the White house). We had so many happy memories there together. I knew him for most of my life, and I am glad he walked with me.

May the road rise to meet you,
May the warm rays of sun fall upon your home,
And may the hand of a friend always be near. ...
until we meet again.

Printed in the United States
by Baker & Taylor Publisher Services